LIFE
made
SIMPLE

Secrets to Wealth & Happiness
Hidden In Plain Sight

This book is dedicated to the love of my
life and my best friend. This book would not have
been possible without you.

LIFE
made
SIMPLE

Secrets to Wealth & Happiness
Hidden In Plain Sight

JOE COX, Jr.

Life Made Simple Books LLC
5916 East Lake Parkway Suite 158
McDonough, Ga. 30253
LifeMadeSimpleFeedback@gmail.com

Cover wrap design by Leah Kanuho
Illustration by Joe Cox Jr.

Library of Congress Cataloging in Publication data

ISBN 978-1-961655-00-3 Paperback

ISBN 978-1-961655-01-0 Hardcover

ISBN 978-1-961655-02-7 eBook

Cox, Jr. Joe

1.Self-Help   2. Happiness 3. Wealth 4. BodyMind 5. Personal Growth. 6. Self-Healing 7. Spiritual Healing I. Title

All rights reserved. Printed in the United States of America

The publication is designed to tell my story to provide relevant information from a life lived without direction. This is the author's interpretation of the life process and actions he needed to find wealth and happiness in his life. This is not psychological, financial or legal services. Its for educational and entertainment purposes only. The medical conditions discussed should only be cared for under the directions of a physician. Proper care from a physician should not be avoided, delayed or discarded when there is reason to consult a physicians. There may be come ides in the book that may not agree with allopathic med- icine. This book is not designed to diagnose, treat or prescribe any disease. The author accepts no responsibly for such use. – Joe Cox Jr.

Author Buy Back Guarantee

The author offers a 90-day guarantee on any retail purchase of this book. His main objective in sharing these principles of success is to facilitate their implementation in the lives of readers to help each one create their best life.

Promotional program guidelines:

1. If you do not find the principles taught in this book to be effective, you may return the printed copy within the first 90 days of purchase to the address listed below for a full refund.

2. Your copy must have been purchased new through a retailer or online distributor.

3. A copy of the original receipt must accompany the return along with the identification of the refund recipient, with email and phone number. One refund per customer.

4. We ask, as a courtesy, that you also include a short written statement regarding why you are returning the book. The return is unconditional providing all return policies are followed.

5. The returned copy must be unmarked and undamaged and in resalable condition.

6. We accept no responsibility for books mailed* and not received.

Mail To Address:

Life Made Simple Books LLC
5916 East Lake Parkway Suite 158
McDonough, GA 30253
LifeMadeSimpleFeedback@gmail.com

This buyback program is not associated with or implemented by the printer, distributor, or retail outlet. We release all retail outlets and the distributor of any liability in this promotional program offered by the author. The author is solely responsible for this program.

*We recommend using a registered or certified mailing service.

Table of Contents

CHAPTER 1

The Beginning of Greatness

There was a child who grew up in a very broken home. It was a toxic environment, mentally and emotionally abusive. He grew up feeling lost, hopeless, and confused, disconnected from the world.

His father was an alcoholic, seldom around, too busy fulfilling his own wants, lust, and desires of the world to notice the needs of his young son but instead reinforced his son's sense of abandonment.

His mother, a verbally abusive person, saw her child as a possession, something to be controlled, lashing out in anger over his mere existence as if he were the mirror image of her husband and everything she hated.

The boy suppressed his feelings and emotions; depression was the only life he knew. Self-loathing was his comfort zone. Not allowed to learn and play freely as a child should, his spirit broken, carrying burdens no child should endure.

His home was a place of chaos. His parents' routine bickering and screaming quickly turned into violent arguments, a battlefield of verbal attacks. Through tears, he shielded his younger siblings from flying objects. Deep down, he knew this behavior was wrong.

Any questioning regarding his world made him the target of his mother's rage. She would scream that he was ungrateful for all that she had done for him, her insults flung at him like daggers, continuing to chip away at his spirit, one word at a time.

He was trapped, forced to hear her say, over and over, a daily confirmation, that he would never amount to anything. He knew he was unwanted. She would remind him that he was the reason she was in "this mess", as though his existence was a curse to the family. He could not understand why he was so flawed, broken, and unlovable.

He attempted to show her his potential. Each effort for approval was met with discouragement, resulting in his defeat and the feeling that he would always lose. She would make sure of it.

His attempts at accomplishments were always met with the same response, his mother's laughter, and words that seemed to seal his fate. "No matter what you do, I'll never be proud of you," robbing him of any spark left in his eyes. He was dying inside. With continued rejection, in a world where he could not win, his future held little hope. "Why continue?" that voice in his head would say.

At thirteen, the divorce came. Knowing things would change, he hoped it would be for the better, but things got worse. He became a prisoner in his own home. His mother demanded that he take on the burdens of the father he never saw anymore. No sports, no friends, no time to be a teenager. Too much yard work, dishes, and babysitting to be done. His inner fight no longer seemed to matter.

His mother had a new goal: to find a replacement husband. She was gone for hours at a time, leaving him at home watching over the three younger siblings, two still in diapers.

Despair engulfed him, his life force ever decreasing day by day, his needs totally ignored. No joy. No happiness. No hope. The emotional turmoil was debilitating. Television was his only outlet to the world. As he grew, so did his misery. He wished he had never been born. He felt like everyone would have been better off that way.

Life at school was no better. He was too introverted for conversation. Being bullied and harassed reinforced his feelings of being unwanted and unlovable. He was always the last one picked for anything. Nobody wanted him on their team. Teachers labeled him "a good kid" but saw him as disconnected, shy, and a slow learner with little drive. He was quiet, never raising his hand for fear of displaying his ignorance.

The world he knew was a place in which he did not belong. To escape, he would daydream of another place, far from that life, a world where he was worthy of love. A place where he was wanted. He didn't know why God hated him so much that he would be punished with a family that did not want him, and with no one to turn to.

He wanted to be like the other kids, with stylish clothes, playing sports, and having school friends. His mother reminded him that she would not tolerate "such selfishness". Forced isolation was taking its toll on him.

He had a feeling that there was more to life but was shut down at every attempt to find it. He seemed destined for sadness. His mother reinforced the idea daily, saying, "You will only grow up to be sorry like your father." His only childhood aspiration was survival.

At fifteen years old, still timid and undernourished, he had a growth spurt, and soon physically towered over his mother. Around the same time, she began allowing him to attend church. He finally had an outlet and a chance to be with kids his age.

He lacked social skills, always unsure of how to interact with his peers. He tried his best despite having no role model. He had no supportive adult from his family or church to guide him. He was left to interpret the world on his own.

Without his knowledge, his mother intervened in his potential friendships, to force her narrative on the other boys, undermining any potential bonding opportunity for her son. Sabotaging gave her control and so her threatening behavior continued.

Soon, he was invited to a dance. He had little knowledge of dancing, but he attended anyway, and a girl caught his eye. He wanted to talk to her, maybe ask for a slow dance. Fear flooded his body. He thought, *But what if she says no*? Building up the courage, he asked her, with a gentle smile, she said yes!

Something was different about this girl. When around her, a light of confidence came over him. It was a new feeling for him, the feeling that he mattered. Her attention, the way she looked at him, he had never experienced anything like it before. With her, he felt like *someone.* She had a gentleness that he had never known existed on earth. The smile of an angel radiated from her face.

Excited to share the experience and feeling on top of the world, he told his mother of this girl, believing that she would now see him as worthy of love. He would no longer be a nobody. He needed to believe his mother would see his value.

His mother simply replied, "You are not worthy of a girl like that." and she turned and walked away. Her words pulled him right back into his reality of self-hatred and unworthiness. All hope drained from him. Devastated, he began to accept the mindset he had been conditioned to believe that he was worthless. His toxic programming insisted that his mother must be right; such a girl would be cursed to have him.

The years of reinforced inadequacy had sealed his fate, concreting him into nothingness. A zero. He had no choice but to let go of the thought of her.

He saw her from time to time, but he never asked her out, though she was always on his mind. As the years went by, he wondered what had become of that angel, the one that made him come alive inside. He was left to carry the baggage of his perceived worthlessness into adulthood.

By age 16, his toxic home life had taken its toll and he reached his breaking point. Living on the street would be a better option. He packed his bags and left, his mother's last words to him ringing out as she screamed, "See - I was right! You're just as sorry as your father, running away from your problems! You will never amount to anything!"

Is there a positive future for this boy? Is it possible this child will experience wealth, happiness, and love? Or will he have children only to become the abuser, and repeat the dysfunction?

Statistics indicate that he will likely go through life angry and bitter, seeing himself as a victim, a sense of worthlessness dominating every thought, carrying fear and lack into every part of his life. When good things do happen, they will scare him, so he'll reject anything outside his comfort zone and resort to self-sabotage. He will likely allow feelings of shame and guilt to dominate him. He may suppress his emotions and feelings of self-disgust by numbing himself through addictions to get relief, and will likely end up an alcoholic, drug addict, homeless, in jail, or worse.

Childhood is the time the Divine has set aside for us to prepare for adult life in love, nurturing, guidance, and protection. Many of us did not receive what we needed in childhood. This child is ill-prepared mentally, emotionally, and spiritually. Without the necessary tools and skills, is it possible for this child to experience a fulfilled life? I will show you that anyone, no matter their background, can find the healing they need to live in love and harmony as they come to understand how life works.

How do I know that? Because I was that child.

CHAPTER 2

Making Life Simple

Today, I live in a state of wholeness in all I do. Happiness follows me everywhere I go. How is that possible? How is it that a child so misguided and unloved could find harmony within himself to live a life of joy, peace, and happiness when many others struggle with bitterness, anger, self-loathing, or a victim mentality, no matter their background?

Perspective is two people looking at the same thing from two different viewpoints, each seeing something completely different. Example: You can have a rainy day, 40 degrees outside. One person says how cold and damp it is and how they think they are coming down with a cold because of it, complaining that they hate days like this. Another person has gratitude, knowing we need rain for the trees and plants. They see the weather as an opportunity, not to work outside but to have a day of rest, a day to stay inside by the fire and read or spend time with family.

My perspective made all the difference to my outcome. It's up to each one of us to see the good in everything. Life is how we see it. We each create our own reality. We just need to understand how the game of life is played.

I now maintain a life balance that few ever find. Living in a state of happiness includes living in love, harmony, and abundance in all things. I want to share what I have learned with the rest of the world. My goal was to create a guide for taking simple, fundamental steps to create the life you desire, no matter your background.

Life is simple. We tend to complicate it when we are confused about the proper steps to take. We are not meant to guess our way through life. We need clarity of purpose, meaning, and an understanding of how to attain happiness. Confusion is where all darkness begins. Darkness is trying to paddle upstream, against the current, resisting and fighting life. Clarity is paddling downstream, with the current, accepting life, guiding yourself from side to side, and creating and designing your life one decision at a time.

Happiness does not happen overnight. We also cannot think our way to happiness. I tried that approach for years. There is a reason it does not work. I will show you the secret of happiness that has been hidden in plain sight, but first, let's set the foundation.

Awareness through clarity is required for happiness. Most people lack awareness because of the many distractions and numbing devices that keep us blind. Distractions allow us to be controlled and manipulated, keeping us from our potential.

Life is all about how you perceive it. The goal of this book is to give you clarity, so you can gain awareness and become the person you were born to be.

Backstory Continued...

After I packed my bags and left my mother's home, I moved in with my grandmother Cox in her cinder block basement. She could not believe I was willing to live downstairs in those conditions. It had no heat or cooling. It had a concrete floor, no windows, one light bulb, and one electrical outlet, but I didn't care. I loved it. It was quiet. It gave my head some of the peace it had never had before.

I was about to start my junior year of high school and switched schools, hoping to get a fresh start. For me, quitting school was never an option. I vividly remember my first day at the new school. My grandmother had gotten up and fixed me a balanced breakfast before she went to work. Eggs, sausage, grits (it's a southern thing), and toast. I realized then that I had never had a full breakfast before school.

My grandmother was a very kind woman. Looking back, I can see the fight she'd had in her past. My grandfather had been an abuser. She was now on her own dealing with her divorce the best way she knew how. Her kindness inspired me. I saw the difference it made in my life, so it became my goal to be kind to others. She didn't know how to help me with the junk in my head. So, I continued my struggle, trying to figure it out.

I had no supervision. I was making all my own life decisions. Being completely responsible for myself was healthy for me. I began coming out of my shell. I got an after-school job. I made some genuine friends for the first time. With good food in my stomach, a good night's sleep, and toxic screaming out of my life, my grades shot up. I was engaged at school. My desire for learning increased. I took an auto shop class and cars became my outlet. Without me knowing it, my healing journey had begun. I found a good job that kept me busy and productive. I volunteered to go to summer school to make sure I graduated on time. On graduation day, neither of my parents showed up.

I could have dropped out of high school, but I stayed and graduated because I wanted more from life. I didn't do it for my parents or anyone else; I did it for me. I graduated high school reading and writing at a fifth-grade level. Still confused, lost, and very ill-prepared, I was guessing my way through adult life.

> *You either control your mind*
> *or your mind will control you.*
> *It's your choice.*
>
> Joe Cox, Jr.

Choosing a Path

I didn't feel that I was anything like my parents. While we receive DNA from our parents, we are all separate, independent beings. We often adopt the behaviors of the people that surround us during childhood, accepting their belief systems about life, but we do not inherit their behaviors. We choose our behaviors. We choose our character. We choose our personalities. We can choose whether to repeat dysfunctional behavior or not. We choose how we respond to our circumstances. We can choose any type of life we want.

I felt I had potential, but I didn't know the next step to take. My poor learning skills were due to my toxic family environment, not limited abilities, but I didn't understand that at the time. I didn't understand that my past did not have to determine my future. I was afraid of everything. All I knew was I didn't have the answers. Two benefits of understanding that you don't have the answers are self-awareness and an open mind. It is the close-minded person, the one that quits school, the one that is not teachable, the one thinking they have all the answers, who is doomed.

I wanted knowledge from people who had accomplished what I wanted to accomplish. I began to read. One of the first books to help me was from the great Les Brown, who asked, *"How hungry are you?"* He was asking how badly I wanted a better life. I was starving for answers. His question prompted independent thinking. I knew I wanted it and I was willing to do what it took to get it. I just didn't know where to start.

Decision-Making Skills

I needed something to help guide me to make good decisions. Looking at my parents' lives, everything was confusing, chaotic, toxic, and self-serving. Their choices created those results. My parents made horrible choices and life gave them natural consequences.

How could I make good decisions in life when I had never been taught how? I devised a system to make good decisions.

I decided to question every decision in my life. I would ask myself, *What would my parents do*? Then I would do the opposite. It was a trial-and-error approach, but it worked. Opposite choices gave opposite results. This new approach to decision-making was life-changing. It helped me get started on a better path.

Learning to Play the Game of Life

Knowing what happiness is and taking the steps to attain it allows the magic to begin. There are laws both seen and unseen that regulate balance in life. We will call these "the rules to the game of life". These rules are as valid as gravity. You may not realize it, but they are at work in your life. Have you ever played a game with someone who was not playing by the rules? How did that work out for them in the long run? Not knowing the rules is not an excuse. I am going to show you how to play the game of life to win.

I learned many of these rules of life by testing them. These rules are guardrails to guide you on your life's path. They keep you on the most beneficial path for you if you have the awareness to follow them. They can keep you balanced in your thinking. Ignore the rules, and you will be out of harmony, out of alignment, and out of balance with life, and in turn, you will attract all the things you don't want. This is why so many people who live by the seat of their pants live in dysfunction and chaos. We need balance and structure in all things.

If you believe you are on this planet merely to eat, work, sleep, and have fun and pleasure, you are missing out. A life focused on fun and pleasure is a life of suffering, a life of addictions. A life of meaning and purpose leads you away from suffering and into happiness.

A life of meaning and purpose
leads you away from suffering and
away from addictions.

Joe Cox, Jr.

Today, I have a beautiful extended family and a wonderful wife. I am surrounded by high-level, high-energy people. I repel people that are toxic to my being. I live with peace in my heart and abundance everywhere I go. I only send love to the outside world, living without regret. Life is simple once you understand it. I did not create this life by chance; it was attracted to me through my intentions, thoughts, and actions.

Moving Beyond a Dysfunctional Past

Many people have lived through childhood dysfunction or a toxic relationship that resulted in some type of trauma. Past trauma creates a weak foundation for making sound choices in the future. As children, we have few choices. As adults, we have the means and power to heal. Poor choices lead to hardship. From each hardship comes a lesson. If we had known the life lesson in advance, we would not have had the hardship.

We are required under the laws and rules of life to learn our lessons before moving forward. People may test us, but life is not here to test us - it is here to teach us. How many people keep doing the same things and get the same result, then complain rather than change their choices and behaviors?

Chances are any suppressed or repressed trauma or child-hood dysfunction will continue to revisit us until we address it and release it from our being. Denial does not work. I tried that. Attempts to ignore it, repress it, or try anything but face it will get you stuck in life, and it will come back as a break-down, depression, a midlife crisis, anxiety, or other mental or emotional struggles. Even worse, left unattended it could manifest through the body making you mentally or physically ill. I will share with you how I healed in future chapters.

Stuck In Life

Sometimes we get stuck in life, unsure of the next step to take. It's a feeling of being trapped and keeps many people from moving forward in life. Getting "stuck" in adulthood is often the result of past emotional turmoil or trauma of some kind. It limits our capacity to properly process emotions and feelings. Many are unable to get past the trauma of growing up feeling unwanted and unloved and now live in lack. They feel stuck in a world of hopelessness but don't understand how to get "unstuck" and start living.

Mixed Signals

Sometimes, we cannot figure out how to get unstuck because of cognitive dissonance. This is when our thoughts, beliefs, or attitudes conflict with one another. This sends us mixed signals. Example: You want more money but either con-sciously or subconsciously believe money is evil, so you are stuck when it comes to money. The opposite of being stuck is having resolve. Having resolve around money means understanding that money is not evil, but the way we attain or use it can be. Your higher power wants you to have abundance.

Another example of mixed signals is when you want to be loved but you don't love yourself. If you rely on the outside world to give you love or define your worthiness, you will always be disappointed. You can never truly give love unless you love yourself. Most of us are going about it backward. I did. I believed I needed someone else to show me love to validate my worthiness. When I reversed my thinking and began to love myself first, things changed. I now define my own self-worth. We will cover in an upcoming chapter how to have unconditional self-love.

The Perfect Childhood

Childhood is meant to prepare us for life, though many of us did not receive proper preparation. Our responses to everything in life are based on our programming from our experiences as children. Trauma can keep a negative loop replaying in our minds. Many people wish they'd had a better childhood.

Let's imagine that everything was perfect in your childhood. You had two loving parents that never yelled, were always positive, always had great jobs, and gave you the exact guidance and support that you needed. There was always money to provide for your needs, and your parents were always available when you needed them. If you'd had such an upbringing, you would have been taught how to prepare your mind, body, and spirit for adulthood. You would know yourself and know what you wanted in life. Sounds great, right? The problem is you have to know darkness to appreciate the light.

The question is, if you didn't know challenges or hardships, or were never betrayed or disappointed, how would you know happiness when you have it? How could you handle a world full of issues to overcome? This might be the reason that spoiled kids are never satisfied, often acting out, rebelling, and causing problems. They want, want, want, with no gratitude. Gratitude and appreciation are two of the fundamental emotions that coexist with happiness.

You Have What It Takes

People who believe the grass is always greener on the other side believe they have little or no control over their own lives. The day you realize that your side is *always* greener is the day you take control of your life.

It's true, most of us have some type of generational dysfunction handed down to us, one generation after another. I have known many who have appeared to have it better than me but later found that they were dealing with tragedy within themselves or their families.

Rather than assuming that everyone has it better than you, look at it this way: life is like playing poker. If a poker player does not like the cards he is dealt, he must decide whether to play the hand or not. If the player knows the rules, knows the statistics, and knows how others play, he can often win even playing with a crappy hand. A wise man can win with almost any hand dealt. That is where the saying comes from, "Play the hand you're dealt in life." I did and I won. You can too.

In life, you're only dealt one hand, but you have a lifetime to play it. The key is to accept your hand. Resisting it only prolongs the suffering. Accept it with enthusiasm, joy, and gratitude. For some, it can be difficult to accept. It was for me, but once I accepted it, it began to change my life. If you think you are going to lose no matter what you do, you're right. You must believe you can win in order to thrive.

Winning is simply understanding how to play life. This book outlines a way to understand life so you can win, but your outcome still depends on your participation. Without taking action and being in flow with the stream of life, this book or any other will not help you.

Only Limitation

We each have a personal belief system, a set of principles that form the basis of one's personal philosophy or moral code regarding society and the world. It is our interpretation of everyday reality. It is how we personally view, understand, and organize life. It determines what we think is right or wrong, true or false, and how things should or should not be.

Roger Bannister was the first person to break the 4-minute mile barrier in track and field on May 6, 1954. Three minutes and 59.4 seconds. Athletes had a mental barrier to the belief that a human being could run a mile in under four minutes. Since it was shown that it could be done, over 1,664 people have done it, including 18 high school students. The fastest 4-minute mile is now 3 minutes 43.13 seconds.

How many people before Bannister believed it could not be done? Who was he following to be able to break that record? No one - he was leading. He was not in competition with the other runners but with himself. He created his own standard. Creating your own standard is believing in yourself in order to control the direction and distance of your life.

Every life has a standard. Sadly, many people default to a very low standard. How did I overcome my childhood? My standards would not allow me to accept a life of anything but abundance in all things and to live a life of happiness through purpose and meaning. What is your standard?

Believe, Conceive, & Achieve

Dr. Joe Dispensa's research on the mind-body connection demonstrates scientific proof that the brain cannot recognize the difference between reality and imagination. If you can conceive it and believe it, you can achieve it. The question is, do you believe in yourself?

Once we believe that something is possible, we can make it a reality.

A New Way to Look at Life

Welcome to Earth School - a new way of looking at life. It seems life has gotten complex and confusing these days. We are placed in situations today that work against our design and we are looking for solutions. Many people are struggling, not sure how to fix their lives, and wondering how they ended up where they are, while others are just getting started, unsure of how to approach life.

Life is nothing more than one big classroom with many teachers. Everyone is your teacher. Your purpose is to learn and grow. You were born the perfect you and now it's time to become the best you.

I believe this book can benefit you at any age or stage in life, no matter your background. Almost everyone is struggling with something. I have found that there are clear solutions for every situation. I will help guide you to find *your* answers.

I have achieved long-term, authentic completeness, whole-ness, and richness resulting in happiness, the type of happiness that our daily issues do not affect. A person can live life, have daily issues, and still live in a harmonious flow and exist in a state of happiness. We need to understand what it will take to get us to that state of happiness and what it takes to stay there. This book will help you do that.

Happiness can be difficult to accomplish from any back-ground, but how can you make it happen if you come from a dysfunctional background? And how is it possible to have long-term happiness in a crazy world like we live in today? Clarity! Clarity in all we do.

A confused mind takes no action. Life's most basic purpose is progress. As a young person, your main goal is to learn as much as possible, then convert your knowledge into wisdom. You begin to gain wisdom when you take action. Too much unapplied knowledge creates confusion. There is a common saying from George Bernard Shaw, "Those that can, do; those who can't, teach." Wisdom is found in doing.

I grew up confused, but my life force began to want more from life. The more I looked for answers, the more motivated I became. The stronger my drive became, the more answers I began to find. Through action, I gained wisdom.

> ### *Knowledge is a person explaining a complex issue.*
> ### *Wisdom is a person showing you how simple it is.*
>
> *Joe Cox, Jr.*

Lessons Learned

Sports are a good way for many kids to learn teamwork and bond with friends. Those skills can also be utilized throughout life. My growth was limited. I was never allowed to participate in traditional sports or band activities. I didn't get a chance to build those social skills in childhood. I never received a trophy like most other kids.

Once I was on my own, I turned my negatives into positives. Today, I am grateful I never received a trophy or award as a child because it reminded me daily that I was the underdog in everything I did. It instilled in me a determination for achievement that kept me going when all the chips were down. I had to try harder, work harder, study harder, and do the things most others were not willing to do. "It's not fair" was not in my vocabulary. Failure was not an option. My motivation was to make sure the chaos of my past did not repeat and control my future. The most important principle I learned is to never, ever give up.

I quickly learned that the most expensive advice is free advice. I was given all the free advice I didn't want. I was told I was not "college material." I was encouraged to get a steady job on an assembly line. Deep inside, I wanted more; I just didn't know where to start.

Two of the first and most important lessons I have learned in life are, first: *Don't listen to foolish people.* I stopped listening to a poor man's advice on how to become rich and a miserable person's advice on how to be happy. The second lesson: *Question everything.*

Beneficial information brings us closer to balance, harmony, and alignment. It is our responsibility to find and apply it. I already knew unbeneficial information creates a victimhood mentality which leads to self-destruction. I looked for what was going to make me mentally and emotionally stronger. I recommend you do the same.

Learning By Living

At 18 years old, we are all lost to some extent. We are just beginning to live life. You don't learn how to live and then live. You learn how to live by living, learning daily lessons. Life requires on-the-job training.

I challenge you to test the principles in this book and decide for yourself if they are true. I believe my life experiences provide relevant insights that will help guide you in your journey. I did something few people do - I took risks. Calculated risk! I messed up and made mistakes over and over again without regret because I knew I could never fail. I gained experience in every area of knowledge I could, and over time I learned from each mistake. One of my best decisions was to remove the word "failure" from my vocabulary. The fear of failure stops many people cold, but the fear of making a mistake we can handle. In life, you only fail if you don't try, or you give up. In the real world, there are only mistakes, not failures. Without the fear of failure, I was not scared to try. There are some things that cannot be taught in a classroom. *You never have to live a life of suffering if you have the answers, understand them, and take action in alignment with life's rules.*

Will This Book Help You?

There is a reason prosperous families often continue to live in abundance one generation after another. It's not just luck. They have information that most of us are missing. A fundamental truth is that wisdom and knowledge are not the same thing. It was basic knowledge that I needed as a young man so that I could take action to gain wisdom. I have known wealthy people that could barely read and write. I have also known college educated people that were broke. Life is about learning the daily lessons to gain wisdom.

No matter where you are in life, this book will give you an advantage in building a life of happiness with abundance in all you do. I pray that you will benefit from this material as much as I did and still do.

This book is a collection of information that helped me learn ways to live an authentic and abundant life. It contains over

40 years' worth of knowledge and wisdom that I needed when I was young. With this applied information, I now have peace and live in gratitude and appreciation every day. It took much trial and error to find the answers, but I have outlined them here for you.

I am not your typical author. Writing a book was never my goal, but after all these years, I felt inspired and called by my higher self to write this book, as part of my life's greater purpose. This book is written from my heart to yours.

The objective of this book is not to tell you how to live your life but to show you how to find answers to get the results you want. We need teachers to share knowledge, but in truth, you are being taught by everything you do and everyone you meet. It's up to you to have the awareness to look for and gain knowledge from each lesson so you don't repeat the same mistakes.

My guidance is not based on vague theories but on measurable steps. This is how I did it. Everything I share in this book comes from personal experience. I do not have any fancy paperwork on the wall to say I am qualified to tell you how to live your life. I am not a certified expert. While there is much scientific support for what I share here, you will not get that in this book. This is simply my story of how I overcame and thrived to live in a state of happiness. While this book is about my life, it is really about you. How will you get where you want to go in life? You can do it once you have the tools and skills.

Smart people learn from their own mistakes. Wise people learn from others' mistakes. Consider how you can apply these principles to your life. My pain can become your gain.

You can become a game changer. You can rise above any situation. I learned early on that the world owes me nothing. I am not entitled to anything unless I earn it. When I took full responsibility and accountability for myself, that mindset took me to levels of achievement that I never thought possible.

Now let's begin learning about happiness.

CHAPTER 3

This Thing called Happiness

Today we are walking down the streets in the city. We are stopping to talk to everyday folks and asking them, "What do you want in life?" The answer we almost always get is some form of "happiness." Then we ask, "What is happiness?" Most people stop for a moment and get a blank look on their faces while they think about it. If they answer, we seldom get the same answer twice. Most people guess. We find that the majority of people of all ages have a difficult time defining what happiness is. If we don't know what happiness is, how are we going to attain happiness in our lives?

Stop for a minute and ask yourself, "What is happiness to me?" Is happiness a place? Is it a person? Is it something I can hold? A destination? Something in the future?" Do you often think to yourself, "One day I will be happy when...?"

Happiness is the goal for most people, the holy grail of life. Society has taught us that if we are not happy, we must be failing or doing something wrong. Many become depressed, feeling lost, lonely, disconnected, or stuck and not sure which way to go. Why does happiness seem to elude so many of us?

Let's change the question to, "What would make you happy?" Most now respond with "money" or "winning the lottery." If that is true, use your critical thinking skills to consider these scenarios:

> **Scenario 1:** What if you won the lottery and you never had to work again, *but* you had no loving family, no friends, and no real connections? Would you be happy?

Research shows that a state of happiness mainly comes from connections with family and friends, but few people answer that they primarily wish they had better friendships or connections. They typically put money first.

> **Scenario 2:** You won the lottery and never had to work again, *plus* you had loving family and friends. This time, however, you had no goals, no motivation, no accomplishments, and no purpose or meaning. Would you be happy?

Research has also found that accomplishments, meaning, and purpose are also essential components of happiness. Can a person be happy if they question their own value, abilities, and self-worth? Are we chasing what we think will make us happy only to be disappointed when we get it? See where I am going with this? There must be more to happiness than easy money. It seems life satisfaction and family play a major role. In other words, happiness comes from an accumulation of several aspects of life.

The Struggle to Understand Happiness

Many people struggle to get through each day while hoping to reach the destination of happiness "one day". Many of them believe that they will not be happy until retirement. Then they can sit on the beach and drink piña coladas all day. On the surface, it sounds great, but in reality, how would you feel after doing that all day, every day, for a week? A month? It might be fun for a short while, but is that really happiness?

As a young adult, I had a great attitude, worked hard, and achieved many of my goals. By age 35, I had achieved the typical American definition of success - I was a millionaire. But I knew I was still not happy, not even close. I was wealthy but I did not have richness. I had money but I did not have abundance in all things. I was pleased with my accomplishments but not fulfilled. I thought I was "doing it right" but I was not in a state of happiness. I found myself thinking, *What did I do wrong? Is happiness a real thing?*

Fast Forward

Today, I am in a good place in my head and my heart. I figured out what I needed to attain balance in order to attract happiness. I have a thriving career, and the type of marriage that most guys dream of, built on love and trust. That kind of connection does not just randomly happen. I adore my wife. She is always loving and supportive. I also have the support of a new, amazing extended family and quality friends. I have worked for and attained everything my family of origin could not give me. I discovered personal meaning and purpose. I now live a fulfilling and satisfying life.

Being Happy versus Living in a State of Happiness

No matter your life circumstances, you can feel happy in response to a joyful occasion like holding a newborn baby, sharing a moment with someone who cares, or going to a concert with a friend. Being happy fills your spirit for the moment but is fleeting. You can have a happy moment without wholeness, but to live in a state of happiness requires wholeness.

Living in a state of happiness is long-term, more profound, and continuous. This true, authentic happiness comes from within and can only be achieved by first working on and attaining wholeness which is the balance of mind, body, and spirit.

There is a simple way to know whether you are momentarily happy or living in a state of happiness.

After having a happy moment during the day, when you are back home, back in your daily environment, getting ready for bed, take a moment and ask yourself, *Is that peace and harmony that accompanied that happy feeling still with me?* If loneliness, sadness, or emptiness has set in, you still have some imbalance and have not yet attained a state of happiness. However, if you still feel full of peace and harmony most of the time, you have attained happiness.

Thinking of Happiness All Wrong

There are many underlying variables that affect our happiness. It all seems very complex. Happiness is only complex if you don't know how to define happiness. It is simple once you can understand it.

Happiness is what we all desire. If offered, I am confident no one would decline happiness, but many decline the work needed to attract happiness believing there is a shortcut.

My goal is to help you understand happiness and the simple steps necessary to attain it. Like almost everyone else, I had been thinking of happiness all wrong.

The first breakthrough was when I realized I went looking for happiness as if it were lost. I realized if you go looking for happiness you will never find it. That is because happiness cannot be possessed. You can't hold it and it is not a destination.

Happiness is not a thing. You do not *find* happiness, you attract it. It's a balancing act, like balancing a spinning basketball on your fingertip. You must keep it moving. With idleness, the basketball falls, and so will your happiness.

Happiness is simply a byproduct of balance and alignment in several key areas of your life. Through balance in each of these areas, you can attract happiness wherever you go.

Once you know how happiness is created, resilience is much easier and more natural because you are in alignment with the real, authentic, and complete you.

Life changes as you go through challenges and attain growth. If you feel you lost your happiness, you have simply and temporarily lost your balance. Troubleshoot to find the issue.

See which areas of your life are off balance, then correct the issues, and your happiness will return.

Happiness

If you chase it, you will never catch it
because it cannot be caught.
If you try to buy it, you can't
because it cannot be bought.
Happiness is the answer, not the equation.
If you travel near and far you won't find
it because it's not a destination.
The only real way to attain happiness
is to take action, you know,
Then happiness is sure to be everywhere
you go.

Joe Cox, Jr.

Below is a simple formula to illustrate the dynamics of happiness:

Happiness = Wholeness + Richness

Balance in Wholeness is everything within you.

Balance in Richness is everything outside of you.

The definition of happiness is a state of contentment, joy, balance, and fulfillment. The definition of wholeness is a state of being complete and harmonious. The definition of richness is a state of plenty and abundance.

In summary, happiness is being in a state of joy, feeling complete and in harmony with the forces in your life, and having plenty in all you do.

Now that we have a shared idea of what happiness is, let's break down each key factor. Once you understand happiness, it will be like riding a bicycle. You will never forget it because it will be so simple and natural.

Wholeness = Mind Balance +

Body Balance + Spirit Balance

Wholeness is everything within you. The three factors of internal balance related to wholeness are mind, body, and spirit. In the next chapter, we'll begin *your path to happiness by discussing wholeness*.

Balance in All Things
The Goal is to Get Centered

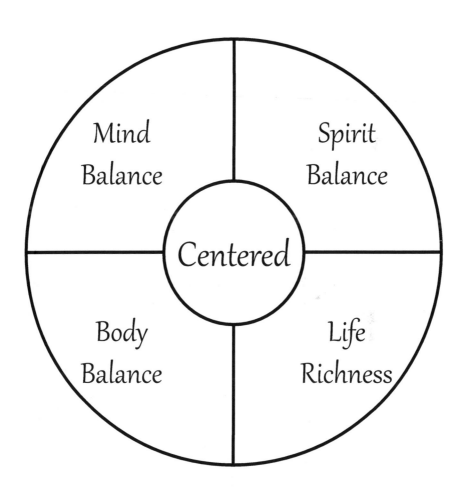

Your Source of Happiness

CHAPTER 4

The Power of Wholeness

We are going to discuss the importance of wholeness and why, without seeking wholeness, chances are we will continue to suffer and struggle in life. Living without seeking wholeness is like trying to hike an unknown wilderness without a compass. We have no direction and nothing to help guide us in life. Wholeness is the most under-emphasized aspect of our lives.

Without wholeness, we can experience loneliness and a disconnect from our earthly experience. Understanding and gaining wholeness is what most people are missing. Without a focus on wholeness, life is all but guaranteed to be far more challenging than it needs to be. Understanding how to gain wholeness is the most important part of our existence in this life, yet we seldom have the guidance needed to accomplish it.

What is Wholeness?

Wholeness is having balance within yourself. Balance in wholeness fosters self-love, peace, and clarity. When in a state of wholeness, you feel complete and harmonious within; you feel unbroken, undamaged, being centered and balanced in all things. When you are whole you experience life at a completely different level. Your perception of life changes. Enlightenment begins with your search for wholeness. You live an unlimited life. Wholeness is being connected between the three components of your internal experience here on earth: your mind, body, and spirit.

Wholeness = Mind Balance + Body Balance + Spirit Balance

The opposite of wholeness is confusion, shame, guilt, anger, illness, anxiety, depression, trauma, sickness, dis-ease, and many other feelings and emotions running amuck, living from only the mind and body, guided by the ego. This is the fragmented self, full of pain and trauma. It is your default until you understand how wholeness is attained.

Many times we experience internal unseen pain within but have no idea how to describe it, much less heal it. Understanding where the pain is, what caused it, and how to heal is what most people are lacking today. Most people are walking around disconnected and fragmented from themselves and wonder why they feel so depressed, empty, and lost, with a lack of will to live life to the fullest. That state of being is very limiting.

"Having wholeness" is your mind, body, and spirit being in balance and in harmony with your life energy. Being without balance in wholeness or "not having wholeness" is akin to living in a house built on sand. It's just a matter of time before the house will collapse. Having wholeness is like having your house built on a firm rock foundation. It is your ultimate source of resilience for life. When you are whole, you are operating on a solid footing. Wholeness is your freedom from a life of struggle and suffering. Pain is inevitable. It is part of life. Pain is the lesson. Pain directions you. But ongoing pain, suffering, and struggle are optional. With wholeness, your pain is limited, and suffering and struggle are eliminated.

In this book, we will review how each key component plays a role in your happiness and abundance. Once you understand wholeness you have the ability to heal and find balance in all things. Once you are in harmony with life, it attracts abundance in all things, including happiness.

How Does Wholeness Play a Role in Your Life?

Many people believe that we are just a body and we are here to eat, sleep, and have fun. Many believe pleasure and fun is the key to happiness. That perspective is operating from the body and the mind which is the ego. Operating from that perspective will leave you detached from your genuine and authentic self. It will leave you feeling the need to numb yourself from reality. Balance in mind, body, and spirit is key to understanding addictions.

Self-care is imperative for wholeness. It is the root of wholeness and everything good in your life. Seeking wholeness welcomes clarity in all things. Clarity results in you attaining the level of courage, compassion, and connection needed to rise above all situations in life.

What is Wholeness?

Wholeness is Self-Love.

Wholeness is Self-Care.

Wholeness is Self-Acceptance.

Wholeness is Self-Respect.

Wholeness is Self-Worth.

Wholeness is Living in Balance.

Wholeness is Living in Harmony.

Wholeness is Living in Truth.

Wholeness is Connection.

Wholeness is Forgiveness.

Wholeness is Peace Within.

Wholeness is the Goal.

Wholeness is Only Found in Self

With Wholeness, Happiness is Yours.

Joe Cox, Jr.

Self-love is also required for wholeness. It is living from the heart. Self-focus is not the same as self-love. Both put themselves first, but the difference is the energy by which they place themselves first. People who are self-focused live from the ego and place themselves first at the expense of others. This approach is living a shallow life. A person with self-love lives from the spirit and places themselves first so they can take care of others.

Benefits of Wholeness

When you are whole, life is simple. Being whole means you are balanced with a well-regulated belief system and a connection to your higher self that provides clarity in all you do. With wholeness, all your daily choices are based on stable emotions and feelings relative to your solid belief system. Your level of wholeness is manifested daily through your body by your intentions, motives, and actions, giving you the results of your choices. Living in wholeness results in you living in peace and harmony to become your best self.

Living Without Wholeness

Feeling out of control and having little hope for the future comes from unhealthy and out-of-balance thought patterns. These thoughts come from confusion. All confusion comes from darkness which is a lack of wholeness.

Past trauma, neglect, and abuse do not make us stronger. They make us angry, bitter, fearful, and insecure and imply that we are not in control of our lives. Such feelings are unnatural to our spirits. We cannot reconcile the concepts of abuse, neglect, rejection, or abandonment. Confusion creates a platform for poor choices and a disconnect from your higher self. Poor choices are the result of a toxic belief system built on a fragmented self.

Most people are suffering from deep emotional pain, unsure of how to interpret life. If we don't know what is causing our pain, we can't heal it and it eventually evolves into suffering. As a solution to our immediate needs, we often seek temporary relief by medicating or numbing our physical, mental, and spiritual symptoms in order to survive.

We need to know the root problem in order to fix any issue. If we know what is causing our suffering we can take action to gain wholeness to be free from pain and suffering.

This book is designed to help you recognize the origins of any imbalances in your life and the path to healing so you can live a fulfilling life.

Homeostasis Through Wholeness

As an adult, your goal is to be whole, to be in homeostasis. Homeostasis is defined as the tendency towards an equilibrium between interdependent elements. This is a state of balance among all the systems needed for you to survive and function properly. Homeostasis is balance in all things.

Core Self

To live in a state of happiness requires wholeness. To have wholeness, you must have a belief system that is in harmony with your core self. The core self is who you were the day you were born into this world.

The day you were born you were whole, complete, perfect in nature. You had the highest level of consciousness. You were in perfect harmony and homeostasis with the self. It was built into that little person to know every necessary thing - how to breathe, how to signal the need for food, etc. With parents that were whole love would provide the rest.

As a newborn, you were completely vulnerable in an unsafe world. Parents living in wholeness naturally and unconsciously have an unseen connection to their baby and are able to provide everything the baby needs to get them started in life. The parents' job is to make sure the baby feels safe in a world where it currently is unable to protect itself.

As a tiny human, you knew self-love and accepted yourself unconditionally. As we grow, depending on our environment, without the proper guidance, life tends to disconnect us from our authentic core selves. Without a proper supportive, loving environment, we could become fearful, growing up to believe we are still in an unsafe world unable to protect ourselves. It is our job to get to know ourselves again, our authentic selves, so we can regain that wholeness, to live life without fear.

Belief System

As you grew, you attained a belief system. Your belief system is a set of principles that together form the basis of your personal philosophy or moral code about society and the world. It is what you define as your virtues or a lack thereof. It is your interpretation of everyday reality and how you personally view, understand, organize, and make sense of this mortal life. It encompasses what you believe is right and wrong, true and false, and what should and should not be. Unable to utilize reasoning and critical thinking skills as a child, you gained your belief system through childhood using emotions and feelings.

When growing up in a family structure that lacked wholeness, life becomes excessively challenging for many, and their perspectives on life become distorted. As an adult, it is imperative you understand *why* you believe what you believe.

As an adult, your belief system was developed in one of two ways. First is the default and most common way many live their lives, by adopting the belief system of their upbringing, repeating the same functional and dysfunctional patterns they grew up seeing and feeling. This approach is seldom in line with an individual's core self. Not questioning the "why" behind one's beliefs, creates a hollow human that is just a follower in life. This type of person lives in fear and anxiety and welcomes many other imbalances.

This blind approach leads you away from the self. By adopting a belief system that is not your own, you are living someone else's life and out of harmony with your core self. Accepting beliefs without assessing their merit is a sign of an immature and emotional belief system.

A belief system from childhood that is only made up of emotions and feelings which typically results in foolish decisions. The ego encourages ignorance and taking the easy way in life. This emotion-based belief system is typically adopted by co-dependents, narcissists, abusers, and other lost and confused people out of touch with who they really are. The ego wants rights at the expense of your authentic self. This is a belief system that leads to division and controlling behavior.

Accepting any belief without first questioning it sends you out of harmony and vibration with yourself. You must be able to mesh your core self with your own beliefs. The ego does not want you to question it because it wants to be in the driver's seat of your belief system and your life.

The second and proper belief system takes work but is the most beneficial. It is where wholeness is found. This is finding your authentic self. It takes a desire to know who you really are. This belief system is self-created as you determine your beliefs for yourself.

Many test this in their adolescence in what we sometimes refer to as a "rebellious stage." Rebelliousness is the ego trying to break out of any limitations. This is when it is important to understand what is guiding you to your own belief system. Wholeness is found through intuition.

You begin to understand who you are and get to know your authentic self by laying claim to your own belief system as you examine and assess everything you accept into your belief system. A reason and resolve correspond with every belief you adopt. Defining your own belief system is your ticket to a connection to self, authenticity, and wholeness.

These two different approaches to establishing a belief system result in radically different paths in life. They operate at different ends of the spectrum.

Looking for Yourself

When people begin to realize something is not right in their life and they go "looking for themselves". This is a good thing. This is the beginning of questioning beliefs. Establishing your own belief system and finding balance in wholeness is finding yourself.

In looking for yourself you are seeking truth. Truth is your benchmark for all things. It's a system of order, harmony, and discipline. Having a belief system with a focus on wholeness will open your life to abundance in all things. Truth welcomes compassion and love through your connection to your intuition. This connection allows forgiveness and welcomes acceptance and togetherness. This openness to connection also requires boundaries to limit toxic energy in your life.

Living with Wholeness

To cultivate wholeness is to wake up in the morning not just believing you are enough but *knowing* you are enough. This is a life without resentment, anger, bitterness, envy, or any other toxic emotions or the energy that accompanies them.

The goal is to wake up excited to take on the challenges of a new day. It is living in a state of fullness and balance, never questioning your own self-worth, knowing you are a divine being, always seeking to discover your meaning and purpose, and always looking for the lesson of the day.

In wholeness, you are the authority over the ego and in control of the urges and impulses of the flesh. You are self-disciplined in thought and action. In wholeness, good habits are not a struggle. They come more naturally and easily. They become your way of life. Once everything is in alignment with self, you will thrive in life and happiness will be yours.

Importance of Wholeness

Simply put, when you are in a state of wholeness you attract prosperity and abundance in all you do, resulting in richness, and a life away from suffering and struggling. Life is never easy but, with wholeness, life is not confusing or complex. It becomes simple.

With wholeness, you skip many of the typical lessons and setbacks in life. We all experience obstacles and roadblocks as part of growth and learning. You will learn how to bypass roadblocks and overcome obstacles. When working on your wholeness, you are in the express lane to happiness and abundance.

What is Meant by Balance

Wholeness is balance in mind, body, and spirit. Wholeness naturally seeks homeostasis. Without balance in each of these areas, we will suffer and struggle and attract more pain than necessary. What we are required to do as part of life is to seek a natural balance in all things. These are not opposing forces. Our beliefs, actions, thoughts, and behaviors are the opposing forces when they are misguided. In other words, we are the ones that get in our own way to achieving balance. Getting out of your own way is sometimes the best advice.

How we interpret our experiences here either allows alignment of our minds, body, and spirits with self or we create the negative energy to remain out of balance. As you balance one key component, it will contribute to balancing the other two components more easily, until all three are harmoniously aligned. The first sign that you are approaching this stage of harmonious living is that peace becomes a daily occurrence. Peace is a byproduct of harmonious living.

What is Trauma?

Dr. Gabor Mate said it best in his book The Myth of Normal, "Trauma is not what happens to you but what happens inside you, from what happens to you." Wholeness involves everything within you. You are born with wholeness. Trauma happens throughout life and knocks your wholeness out of balance. Trauma is held in the spirit body and manifests through the mind and physical body. Trauma is nothing more than toxic energy trapped within you, sometimes fragmenting as coping mechanisms. So, how do you fix the trauma? Can you get the trauma released? Yes. Keep reading!

Many people are struggling, without answers, wondering why life is so difficult. Trauma is a major deterrent to our ability to balance our wholeness due to its negative energy stored within us. You can't create a beautiful future by looking through the lens of the past.

While trauma is devastating to our being, there is a process of releasing that toxic energy once we stop fighting it and look for the lesson of each emotion behind the trauma. There are means of releasing the trauma and healing. What if I told you that you could release your trauma and live a beautiful life without revisiting the trauma itself? That is what I did. This book will show you how to do it, but first, you have to want to heal. You must understand why you feel the way you feel. Believe that healing is possible, and then take action. I found a process that released my trauma and allowed me to heal. This process is an amazing, mostly unknown healing method. We are going to discuss this more in-depth in a future chapter. First, it is important to understand how to find your balance in all things.

Where is Happiness?

This book is about knowing where happiness originates and how to attract happiness in your life. Once you balance your fundamental elements, you can receive drastic healing moments within yourself. We look for happiness as if its lost. Happiness is not lost - we are lost. Once we find ourselves and gain balance, we can attract happiness wherever we go.

You can finally stop looking for all the "get rich quick" schemes; betting on horrible odds with the lottery; and the "lose weight overnight" diets.

By now you should know such schemes target your desperation of lack to push you to purchase something. No one can magically help you. You must take the required steps to achieve your goals. This book will show you how it all comes together, but you still have to do the work. Several pieces of your puzzle are missing, and I am going to show you where to find them.

The key is to invest in yourself. I can always tell you the best place to invest your money. Invest in YOU! You are your best lottery. Start by investing in your healing and living in truth.

You are a goldmine waiting to be discovered, and only you can find it.

Creating an Environment for Manifesting

Have you heard of manifesting? Many people attempt to manifest things in their lives without success. The missing link is a connection to intuition. Intuition is the path to your inner connection and self. Sending pure intent from the spirit. Intuition is the energy behind manifesting and receiving.

You have seen others living a beautiful life. How does all that happen? People with a victim mindset would say it was just luck. Luck is an excuse people make when they haven't found their answers.

For manifesting to work properly, seek your wholeness first. Manifesting works in the most immaculate way with wholeness. Wholeness places you in harmony with what you manifest.

You will never have true, authentic happiness or manifest the things that fulfill you most without seeking wholeness. It is the key to internal bliss. Make attaining balance in wholeness your life's mission. Once you begin working on attaining wholeness, the balancing act happens naturally. Seek your wholeness so amazing things can happen to you through manifesting. All things will be open unto you.

Final Thoughts on Wholeness

Many of our feelings of detachment and disconnection are a result of our interpretation of life. We tend to interpret our current experiences through the lens of our past conscious and unconscious experiences. You will never have the future you want until you get a new lens. Working to gain wholeness is your new lens of clarity. With the information in this book, you will have all the tools you need to attain your desired results.

Wholeness Begins with Kindness. Kindness Places You in Harmony with Wholeness.

Joe Cox, Jr.

The sooner you can gain wholeness, the sooner you can become the person you desire. It is healthy and necessary for your spirit to process grief, anger, sorrow, and all other natural emotions. It's *how* we process our emotions and feelings that can be traumatic. If you get stuck in grief and let it fester into bitterness, you will likely miss the lessons and wisdom to be gained from your experience.

Life itself never punishes; we punish ourselves. We are much harder on ourselves than the laws of nature are. Be kind to yourself and seek wholeness and the future is yours.

In the next chapter, we will discuss what guides your life that will allow you to gain wholeness. Then we'll explore how to gain balance in the three key areas of mind, body, and spirit.

CHAPTER 5

What Guides Your Life?

Did you think that you were put on Earth without any source of guidance? As I said before, we are not made to guess our way through life. While our parents' job is to prepare us for adult life, did you know that you also have a built-in *internal guidance system* that will guide you in everything you do and never steer you wrong?

Many of us lacked sufficient parental guidance to prepare us properly for the adult life that we desire. Parents can only teach what they know, which mainly consists of what they were taught by their parents. This limitation is generational.

Humanity has evolved so much in the last several generations. The strength of our internal guidance system increases and becomes stronger with time because the energy of our collective consciousness has risen. Not knowing about, being connected to, or understanding how to use our internal guidance systems is a big reason why so many people are suffering, struggling, and feeling lost today.

I want to show you just how powerful you are. Your body is very limited compared to your intuition. Having an internal guidance system gives you unlimited power over yourself. Don't be afraid of what you can't do; be more excited by what you *can* do. You have greatness in you but to find it you must seek it out. You will not find it while being entertained or distracted.

I asked at the beginning of this book, *What if you had the power to never make a wrong decision?* Your internal guidance system makes that possible.

If parents are not aware of this power, how can they prepare their children with it, even when they have the best intentions? Without the proper information, suffering and struggle will occur far too often and for far too long. Once we learn how to use our internal guidance systems as a daily habit, and we take action by applying correct principles, we can change everything in our lives for the better. This power can only steer us in the most beneficial way to empower and enlighten our lives. With this information, we then have the ability and power to live in a state of happiness and attract everything we desire in life.

We were born to thrive with abundance in all areas of our lives. Living in abundance leads to a fulfilled life. A fulfilled life happens as we gain clarity for making beneficial decisions.

You have abilities within yourself to do amazing things if you tap into this higher power also known as your superconscious. It is there and given to you by your creator, the same source that makes your heartbeat.

In this age of awareness, we are learning all about our unseen powers to control our lives. As the world gains more awareness, this universal energy rises to meet the demand, thus giving us more control over our lives and our inner world as a whole. It is my belief that highly sensitive people and empaths are very receptive to this ability, they just have a gap of knowledge of understanding and the wisdom of how to apply their ability.

Your Internal Guidance System

Now let's look at your internal guidance system. This system is the power within each of us to always make the proper and most beneficial decisions. Making decisions from only rational or conscious thinking is good but will limit you. But tap into this superconscious power, you have the power to never make an unbeneficial decision again. This allows us to stop making foolish or poor decisions and gain control of our outer world by gaining control of our inner world.

Some people may have problems accessing their internal guidance systems. If you have ill intent or are holding grudges, blaming, envying, or focusing on any negative energy, that negativity will block and limit access to your power. You can't expect your guidance system to guide you in truth and love if you're slothful, deceitful, jealous, living in chaos, or have ulterior motives. You must do your part for it to operate properly and to provide wisdom. When you open your mind and heart and allow love to flow, this power always has your back.

For this power to work for you, seek truth and be authentic in all you do. Live with genuine intent and be kind to those around you. Forgive those that betray you and your guidance system will serve you and guide you to the answers that are available to you by your divine right.

Why do you need to do those things for it to work? Because your internal guidance system is the acting force of consciousness and aligns with your intentions. Positive intent raises your consciousness level. The more elevated your consciousness, the more you are connected to it, and the more in tune your decisions become. Your internal guidance system operates in the spirit of truth, so it can never misguide you. It sees things your conscious mind can't.

The ultimate goal is to communicate with your higher intelligence. We are born with a high consciousness, but Earth life and especially childhood trauma can knock us off our centers, keeping us off balance, and lowering our consciousness, making us think we are broken. You are never broken. We are most often just disconnected and confused.

Once you understand how to use this power, you will have more control of your own life than you ever imagined possible. When you tap into this power, there is little you can't do. With this connection, making the most beneficial decisions for yourself becomes a regular practice.

You can never accomplish true happiness without understanding the power of your internal guidance system. It is the connection to your source. Many people have a good life but feel something is missing. This connection is the missing ingredient for many that few recognize. It is a gift that everyone has access to, but few understand.

Your purpose and goal in life is to be a strong, independent human being, to grow and create the life you desire while connecting to all things in the spirit of oneness. Balance in all things is key. With this connection, your life force increases, your awareness increases, and you gain clarity. High consciousness eliminates loneliness or feeling lost. You may be alone, but you are no longer lonely because you are connected to all through your source; you no longer feel lost because answers and resolve come to you much easier and more naturally .

Activating Your Internal Guidance System

This power has already manifested itself to you, you just may not have realized it. It sends you signals but you may never have been taught how to recognize or interpret them. I am going to show you how to use this power to guide your life. It takes practice and time, but it is a gift available to everyone who seeks it. Hopefully, this is an "Aha!" moment for you!

Most people already have access to their internal guidance systems. Here is the proof:

Have you ever had someone pull you into an unexpected situation, then suddenly you have a "bad gut feeling" that something is not right? Have you ever made a decision that "just feels right?" Have you ever had someone say something and it gave you "the chills?" Have you ever been thinking about someone or something and it gave you a "warm and fuzzy" feeling inside? Sometimes you just know when something is right for you, but you are not sure how you know. Where do all these feelings come from? They're coming from within you, but from where? And why? And for what purpose?

You may have heard the saying, "Trust your gut," or you may have said that you have a "gut feeling," but is that what the gut is used for? Or how about a "hunch" or a "nagging feeling?" But what is a hunch, or a nagging feeling? These are all signs sent by your higher power to guide your life. This power has always been in plain sight. It was only hidden because you did not have the awareness to recognize it. This instinctive knowledge is just the beginning of your power.

Additional signs that you are connected or in touch with your inner self and your source, are that you may have a "flash of clarity," "butterflies," "goosebumps," "a sinking feeling," feelings of peace, or a strong feeling of confidence that you made the right decision.

Abusers, narcissists, and other people with ill intent cannot access this power since they are disconnected from their source. This might explain why they do things that make no sense to people who are connected to the self. This disconnect is why some people can steal and not feel guilty. We would say that they have "no conscience" about the things they do. In truth, their consciousness level is just extremely low, below the level of empathy. They have no connection to the voice inside telling them that stealing is wrong. They live in darkness. The ego controls them. Darkness dominates their emotions, feelings, and actions. This low state of being is their choice.

Looking back, every poor decision I ever made was when I didn't follow my "gut feeling." Most people can relate to this. I didn't understand it at the time. The fact you have these feelings reflects that you are in touch with your source, but you must follow those instincts to receive the benefits. Follow your gut. It won't steer you wrong because that would be against its nature. This is proof that life happens *for* you.

If you believe you are a "good person" but feel lost, or bad things keep happening to you, all you need to do is reach out to your source, that is, your guidance system. Meditation is a great way to make an effort. Invite love and have gratitude while sitting in silence. Learn to forgive. Not sure how to forgive effectively and properly? We will explore the truth behind forgiveness in another chapter.

As an adult, the number one way we get disconnected from our source is by accepting negativity into our lives. Most of our issues are self-inflicted. For example, we accept negativity by using words that degrade ourselves and others. Words are very important. Words are powerful. Your words manifest your future. If you are struggling and you talk to yourself in a negative way, it is time to start working on becoming your own best friend. That is the first thing that needs to change in your life. It is important to be kind to yourself. Be aware that others treat you in the way that you feel about yourself.

We have two bodies, our physical and our spirit bodies. It is believed these two are connected through the pineal gland in the brain. The internal guidance system is part of the spirit body. Your conscious mind is connected to your physical body and accesses the brain. Your spirit body is connected to your subconscious mind and your heart. Your heart is sometimes called your second brain. Your spirit body is your energy. It's the recorder of your life. It is your superconscious that is connected to your source. It is your intuition and the essence of who you are. Raising your consciousness will open up infinite possibilities. That is when true change begins.

This is how our internal connection warns us:

When your physical or spirit body needs something, it will send you signals in the form of either physical or spiritual discomfort. You may feel off or like something is not right. Somehow you will be out of balance. Ignore those signs and the discomfort will grow into physical or emotional pain, or both. Going from discomfort to pain creates a greater imbalance in your life. Ignore those signs and your pain will grow into suffering, creating an even greater imbalance. The level of pain in your life is relative to the level to which you are ignoring the signs that are happening. It is tapping you on your shoulder trying to get your attention. Still ignoring the signs? It can begin to destroy you from the inside out with dis-ease. Everything begins within and will manifest in your body when the body is no longer at ease or healthy. It is now in a state of dis-ease, which means not at ease or in balance.

Dr. Joe Dispensa, MD demonstrates the mind-body connection. He explains how this imbalance can begin with minor physical illness but can lead to cancer or other life-threatening disease if ignored. You only receive what you feel worthy to receive. Overcoming is becoming. You have to show up to go up. Worthiness happens when you show up and do the work. People have the power to cure themselves if they look and listen to the signals.

Don't Fear What You Can't Do.
Be Amazed by What You Can Do.

Joe Cox, Jr.

This is my disclaimer. I am not a doctor. If you are experiencing pain or other chronic health issues you should seek medical help. This information is meant to help you to recognize the signs and know how to help yourself. It is important to be in touch with your mind, body, and spirit. If you look for the signs, they will present themselves. Everyone is responsible for his or her own body and knowing what is going on internally.

Final Summary

For those looking for a shortcut in life, this power will not work because there are no shortcuts. This force cannot be abused because it is based on authenticity and truth. Your higher self is in a different dimension that does not know time or money. It will not help you win the lottery, but it will help guide you to an abundant life on the most beneficial path to make your own fortune from your own accomplishments if that is what you seek. It will help you attract the beneficial things that give you richness and abundance from applying yourself.

The truth can be right in front of you but you may not see it. I utilize this ability to recognize truth and direct my life daily in seeking my answers.

To confirm the existence of this power, we must first consider the power of the mind in the next chapter.

CHAPTER 6

Wholeness of the Mind

Wholeness = (***Mind Balance*** + Body Balance + Spirit Balance)

In this chapter, we will talk about how the mind plays a role in your happiness. Without balance of the mind, it is very difficult to have a productive and satisfying life.

The goal of your mind is to access your belief system using critical thinking and reasoning skills. Then it can direct your life to create balance and harmony by guiding you on the most beneficial path for you. We each have our own path but there are different possibilities along the path you choose. It's like a road with multiple forks. Life is not one big decision, but many small decisions based on the same belief system accumulating into one ultimate path.

Let's visit the way to develop that mind of happiness.

That Voice in Your Head

We all have chatter in our heads. It is imperative we learn to control our minds early in life. The sooner the better. Part of controlling yourself is controlling that chatter. What is the voice in your head telling you?

Ego ~~Runs~~ Ruins Lives

You have two forces attempting to get control of your mind. Which one are you going to allow to be the dominant voice in your head?

Your first choice is the ego. The ego is emotion based. Your ego is that little devil on your shoulder living only for the body, saying, *You don't need school. Stealing feels good. Who cares that it's against your beliefs?* It is the voice that tells you to disrespect others or take what you want. If the ego runs your life, it will ruin your life. It is the negative voice in your head. It is the dark force. Beware of your ego. This is the force of the unconscious and low-conscious mind. It's your default inner voice unless you choose the consciousness of light.

The ego is not your friend. It seeks immediate gratification and wants to have fun at your expense. The ego wants what it wants *now*, no matter the consequences. It is closed-minded and unteachable. The ego wants to control you by controlling everyone around you. It tells you to give up on your goals, to take the easy and fast route in life. The ego is greedy and will betray you. It's lying to you, saying, *You're worthless; don't try; you can't win.* The ego suppresses your conscience to silence any guilt or shame for your actions.

A lazy mind is dominated by the ego through negative self-talk, which chips away at your self-love and awareness, destroying your motivation. The ego wants you to be a slave to your emotions and feelings. It controls you through doubt and insecurity and uses arrogance as false confidence and a facade of strength.

Allowing the Ego to Run Your Life,
Will Ruin Your Life.

Joe Cox, Jr.

The Other Voice

The other voice is your intuition. Your intuition is what you find when you go looking for yourself. This is connection based. Your intuition is always bound by truth. It's non-judgmental, forgiving, and loyal. Your intuition is your best friend and will never betray you.

Your intuition is the angel on your shoulder teaching you love, compassion, patience, and empathy, helping you keep only mutually beneficial people in your life. It always guides you toward a better and more purposeful life. Your intuition protects your spirit from pain and suffering by raising your consciousness level to greater awareness. Your discipline and awareness are required to heed the warnings and guidance of your intuition. In truth, there is no easy way to progress, only a simple way that requires your active participation.

Your Thoughts

You will naturally follow your ego by default unless you consciously choose to follow your intuition. You must choose one or the other; you can't follow both.

It's your responsibility to gain control of your mind with proactive, positive thought patterns. Mental control is the first step toward everything positive and beneficial for your life.

Every thought either serves you or punishes you. Every thought pulls you closer to balance and harmony or sends you closer to chaos. You make decisions based on the options available to you.

You can choose the default path, a path of comfort, entertainment, fun, and ease, the path of a follower to satisfy the ego, living from the body, or you can choose a productive path of learning, growth, and challenges that push your limits and build character and integrity. That is the path of a leader and fosters your personal growth. Either way, your thoughts are in your control.

Clarity in All Things

Mind balance is clarity at its best. It is a state in which you think properly and process information in a healthy, rational way, while still being receptive to creative ideas, utilizing intuition rather than emotions. It's your ability to prioritize things of today and plan for the future while gaining wisdom from the past in an orderly and productive manner. At no time should the mind work against the self, but that is exactly what happens when a mind is out of balance.

A mature, balanced mind always seeks truth because that is where strength is found. Resilience and courage are built on a strong and balanced mind, determined to keep you strong when all else is falling apart around you.

Choosing a Path

No matter what we go through in life, we still have the ability to find balance of mind if we follow life's rules. I had to make many decisions at a young age. At age 16, I had the choice to quit school, join a gang, or just run away. I would not have been missed by my parents and I know they would not have come looking for me.

Instead, I pictured my future, asked my grandmother for a place to stay, and set the stage for my own life. I accepted the responsibility for myself and was forced to quickly mature and not see myself as a victim. I chose to go to summer school two years in a row without guidance. How did I know that was the right choice? I was listening to that voice, my intuition, before I realized what it was.

No matter your background, it is your responsibility to choose your path.

Calm Mind

Learning to quiet the mind is placing the mind in homeostasis. That is why meditation is so healthy. Quieting the mind allows you to be friends with the mind. Friends with yourself. A sick mind is a loud, negative mind run amok. Quiet the mind and look for the lesson.

How you treat yourself determines the level of noise in your mind. Words program the subconscious mind and determine your level of control of the mind. Positive words motivate. The kinder you are to yourself and others, the more you program your mind with positive energy, and the stronger the capacity your mind develops to benefit you.

Calming my own mind, controlling my mental voice, and choosing to follow my intuition were major game-changers for me.

The Emotional Mind

Many people today are self-defeating. They make themselves mentally and emotionally sick through toxic thought patterns that create poor habits. They become their own worst enemies. False beliefs and negativity create a toxic, self-destructive mind. An emotional mind is the mind of the ego. Emotions should stay with the heart, not the mind.

A balanced mind is not ruled by emotions but is constructive and emotionally mature. This is emotional intelligence. It processes emotions by looking for the lesson. When you are in control of your emotions, you are in control of your mind, thus you are in control of your life.

A Mind of Learning

Setting up your life for happiness takes preparation, focus, good habits, and action. It's a mindset. A good mindset is an open mind that connects to your intuition. This process is what creates a life of satisfaction and fulfillment. How your mind processes is the deciding factor. Only you can adopt the right mindset. Order is the secret to a balanced mind. When your mind is organized, your life will have structure.

Would you walk through a construction site without wearing shoes? Why not? Because you have already learned the lesson and saved it in your belief system that construction sites contain many sharp items so walking around barefoot would be hazardous. Step in the wrong place and you would be in instant pain. Poor decisions and foolish actions cause pain. Pain is the lesson. The goal is to learn from your actions and begin making better decisions.

When we seek answers, we are seeking clarity. Seek clarity and you will find yourself. Clarity eliminates fear. We don't fear the things we understand. We fear the things that we ignore. We fear the unknown.

Intellectual and Emotional Maturity

When people operate out of emotion, they are unteachable. People with a victim mindset get their feelings hurt when their mistakes are pointed out. Mature people don't use emotion but rather critical thinking skills in their reactions to others and in making decisions. Maturity accepts criticism as constructive, as a lesson. We must learn to assess our performances objectively. Constructive criticism is given to help you improve.

However, degrading comments are abusive and unacceptable. Bosses and teachers who operate this way have a problem with their own maturity levels. Clarity of the situation will put you in control. Emotions and feelings are meant to help guide us but never control us.

Power of the Mind

I am going to explain in detail how to get your mind to move something. This is a demonstration. "Demo" is Latin, meaning, to point out, or divine power. This is a demonstration of how powerful the mind is:

Take a string or chain with a little weight on the end of it. Most people use what's known as a pendulum. You can find them in any holistic store. Let it hang by two fingers. Focus on its weight at the bottom of the string. Without moving it with your two fingers on top, focus your eyes and mind on it at the bottom at the heaviest part. Now just think of happiness, a joyful occasion, having gratitude in your heart, giving thanks for something, or think of showing gratitude. Just focus your mind and heart with positive and loving energy.

It may take a couple of tries. You will see the pendulum slowly begin to move in a clockwise circle. This is the mind showing you how you can direct spiritual energy to things in the external world through your mind. This is just the beginning of the power of your mind. This is physical proof of manifesting, manifesting in action. If you can get it to move on its own, that is proof you are connected to your intuition. You now know your intuition and your higher power are connected to guide you on a beneficial path in life.

As you get experience with a pendulum, you can ask your intuition questions and it will give you answers, by spinning clockwise for "yes" and counterclockwise for "no". Continue to work on wholeness and you will raise your consciousness allowing the questions to come smoothly and effectively.

That is your connection to your source, your higher self, and your infinite intelligence. You are a powerful being.

If it would help, you can find me on the internet on one or more of the many platforms performing this demonstration.

Your mind is your power. That is why it is so important that you control it. Your mind is your communication to the body through the spirit.

> *Peace is the result of emotions*
> *living in the heart, not in the mind.*
> *The mind controls. The heart understands.*
>
> *Joe Cox, Jr.*

The Best Advice I Can Give

We each have a path in life, and that path will push us to our limits at times. Challenges do not indicate that you are being punished. You are not tested randomly. All experiences are for your growth. Growth happens when you are pushed and you keep going. You may not feel yourself changing at first, but change is happening deep within you.

If you are going through hell in your life, don't stop! Most give up right before the light comes. Keep going until you "see the light". Keep a strong foundation and you will grow out of what you have been through. Remember, your attitude is up to you. You would not be going through a challenge unless it could provide you with a valuable lesson. When you accept your situation in life, then you have the power to change it.

Whatever you resist, persists. This means if you don't accept and learn the lesson, it will recur until you do. Flow with life. To learn the lesson, allow its energy to flow through you. When you resist a lesson, by ignoring it or denying it, you block the energy flow and then absorb and trap the resulting toxic energy. You carry the weight of the resulting emotion wherever you go until you release it.

Allowing the energy to flow in order to release it means identifying the emotional energy as separate from you, then allowing it to flow out of you. We will talk more about this energy release in another chapter. You have limited control of toxic energy once you allow it into your life. If it does not help you, release it. Only accept good energy. You will never have more than what you will accept in life. You will never have more, good or bad, than what you are willing to tolerate.

Rid your life of people who gossip, tend to think negatively, or any other people or things which are toxic or unbeneficial to the mind. Living or operating around narcissists or anyone without critical thinking skills will pull you down. Rid yourself of these types of people. They have their own paths to walk.

Life will not be perfect all the time. Overthinking it is self-sabotaging. Life teaches us through experience, then we test ourselves by pushing the limits. Testing our own limits will naturally involve making mistakes. When something difficult happens in life, avoid the victim mentality of "Why did this happen to me?"

Life Teaches You, People Test You

Many believe God tests them. He never tests, only teaches. He is proud of you. He guides with love, not fear. He wants you to have abundance in all things. You can only have that if you are in control of your mind.

Never *let* another person or situation change your attitude. Let's say you work at a store and a customer is rude to you. Your goal is to *rise above the situation.* Be kind and understanding. Have an "I've got this" attitude.

Have compassion for others but never allow someone to control your reactions. You may apologize for the situation but not lay claim to its negative energy. Avoid saying, "I'm sorry," but instead say, "I apologize for what happened. Let me fix it." See the difference? The difference lies in claiming the negative energy versus allowing the negative energy to flow through and away from you.

You have 100% control over your reaction to life's challenges. You decide whether to have a negative attitude that keeps you limited or a positive attitude that will open the world to you.

The basis for a great attitude is self-care: eat right, get a good night's sleep, and wake up rested, believing you are going to have an amazing day. Be ready for life and look for your lessons each day.

The Results of a Balanced Mind

Be amazed by your potential and never fear the future. You have a phenomenal power within you, but few if any have ever told you that. A strong mind creates a strong life force. A strong life force only sees the life mission at hand and what needs to be accomplished. Your strong will and life force never fears the obstacles, but only see the opportunities. Obstacles will bounce off your armor of resilience. That resilience is your mind, body, and spirit working together to create fortitude. Through that fortitude, you will find the courage to face your challenges, despite fear or pain.

Humans are the only species that punishes themselves over and over again for the same mistake.
A mistake is a lesson - learn from it, then place it in the past where it belongs.

Joe Cox, Jr.

CHAPTER 7

Wholeness of the Body

Wholeness = (*Mind Balance* + **Body Balance** + Soul Balance)

Now let's look at the role your physical *body* plays in your wholeness and in attaining happiness.

As a society, we take our bodies for granted. We tend to see them through the lens of what they are *not* rather than gratefully recognizing what an amazing tool we have been given to live out our mortal lives.

We are too quick to see our bodies as flawed rather than for their capacity to achieve, blind to the vital responsibility of caring for them. Ironically, we are often most critical of our bodies in our youth when they are in peak condition. We tend to neglect and abuse them, sacrificing their future performance potential. We wouldn't purchase a new car and then abuse it. Why do we so often treat our bodies that way?

Body Value

We humans tend to put a dollar value on every physical thing. The easier it is to attain something, the less value we perceive it to have. So, the things we want and don't have must be worth more, right?

We are each given a body free of charge. Consequently, we often assign a low value to our bodies and take them for granted since we made no initial investment. We didn't have to work to gain our bodies — they were a gift. Our only responsibility is to take care of them to facilitate our personal growth.

We recognize the value of *things*, like a new house, motorcycle, or boat, but how we treat our bodies does not always reflect their true value. All too often we treat them as if they are expendable. We often fail to care for ourselves, doing little exercise, and giving our bodies poor diets, drugs, alcohol, etc. If we truly understood the value of our bodies, would we take better care of them?

Let's consider the value of the human body. How would you assign a value to your body? How much money would you take for an arm? A leg? An eye? Would you take a million dollars? Five million? Ten million? What is a fair price? I bet you would say, "I am not for sale." There are some things you can't put a price on.

Congratulations! You are priceless! Now treat your body like you would the most elite sports car you have ever seen. Get your body performing to live the life you were meant to live.

By knowing your value, and the information gathered in this book, you can walk and think like a millionaire, because it's only a matter of time before your bank account is full.

The way we treat our bodies reflects the way we feel about ourselves.

Joe Cox, Jr.

Self-care

Your body is divinely designed. You could say it is the temple that houses your spirit. Few understand the importance of taking care of that machine until it is too late.

We work our whole lives to put money in a bank account, then when we have aged, we are willing to spend it all to gain back our health. Think about that for a moment.

Your body is always changing, always evolving, always growing. First, you grow up, then you grow old. Your body's physical changes are directly impacted by your attitude toward self-care.

Your body naturally and continuously seeks homeostasis. Homeostasis in the physical form is a state of stabilization within your body's systems, creating proper function and equilibrium. Your body, along with your mind and spirit, works to seek that balance in wholeness. Having physical body balance also promotes balance in spirit and mind, the ultimate goal being for body, mind, and spirit to be in mutual harmony.

It is miraculous how we can injure the body and it will heal itself without judgment. That demonstrates that the body naturally seeks a state of balance, an example of physical homeostasis. The body is designed to naturally heal unless we interfere, yet we rarely see that as a miracle. A cut heals without you even thinking about it. A bone mends while just resting. This is proof the body will seek homeostasis, or total balance, if you listen to the body and give it what it needs.

You are the Barrier to your Own Greatness

A barrier is an obstacle to prevent movement or access. You are your own barrier to happiness. The day I realized I was my only barrier to happiness, my life naturally began to change. I finally admitted that all my struggles were due to my focus on how I wanted things to be rather than having gratitude for what was. I had to learn to say, "It is what it is" and mean it, to accept and allow everything and everybody outside of me (my body) to be what it was. My body naturally wanted homeostasis and I was the only thing in the way of that. This shift in mindset was another game-changer for me.

Manifesting

Your body is conductive, made up of mostly water. It continuously communicates with your spirit and mind and the healthier it is and the more in harmony, the better it will communicate. The better you feel, the easier it is to seek and operate in wholeness.

In the last chapter, we demonstrated the power of using the mind to manifest. Another hidden truth is that one's ability to manifest thrives in a healthy and alert body. Manifesting is best done from a state of wholeness and the body plays an important part in that process.

A person that is toxic or intoxicated has very limited ability to manifest. The cleaner and more healed your physical body, the better and more effective manifesting will work for you.

Growth

Your purpose in life is growth. Keep looking, learning, and seeking answers. You send out a vibration of learning when you are seeking answers. Things will begin to fall into place and answers will come to you. Your body is like an antenna for energy. Your physical health has a functional connection to your manifesting.

When you are ready, things will come together for you. As the saying goes, "When the student is ready, the teacher will appear." It is about intention. This is no accident - it is serendipity. Serendipity is the occurrence and development of events by chance in a happy and beneficial way.

Serendipity is common when one is in a vibration of healing. You show intention through your thoughts, behavior, and actions. Seek and you will find. The opportunity will be manifested to you. This allows you to find things you didn't even know were part of your search. This is enlightenment.

Danger of Being Out of Balance

The research is very clear no matter where you look. A simple online search reveals that an estimated 95% of our physical problems come from the way we choose to live. Yet we often blame others for how we feel. It comes down to what we take into our bodies, including food, drink, and all the information we take in through our five senses. The most basic rule is to be intentional regarding anything you eat or drink. To be whole, eat whole foods. Your body is always sending you signals; stay aware and you will live much healthier.

Body Sickness

The purpose of the immune system is not just to get you well when you are sick. That is reactive wellness. The goal is preventive health. To live with intent is to build your immune system to actually prevent you from ever "getting sick." Everything you eat raises or lowers the capacity of your immune system.

There are many holistic, healthy people that are balanced in wholeness and seldom if ever get sick because they live in harmony with themselves. Happiness keeps you well.

When you are sick, you are reacting to an imbalance. Illness is just a lesson, a signal from your body that it is out of balance. In that case, your immune system is not working at its premium level. It is not in homeostasis.

When you have body awareness, and you listen to your body, you will know what to do to become balanced in all things. Wellness will become a way of life.

True Body Health

You cannot look at a person and conclude their level of health. The best way to truly understand one's physical body health is to get a body "report card", which is a full blood workup. These results are objective and do not lie. No matter how your physical body appears, your report card tells the truth. Wholeness is found in truth. When you know the truth, you can establish an effective game plan for your health. Find out the actions you need to take to get and stay healthy. Keep your blood in balance to maintain a healthy body.

Keeping the body whole and healthy is an important step in body balance. Everything you put in your body either contributes to or takes away from your health. The more naturally you eat, the better. Consult with a nutritionist or doctor of functional medicine regarding proper foods and supplements.

Let food be thy medicine and medicine be thy food.
Hippocrates

If you need to take a pill, understand *why* you're taking it. Find out if you are solving the problem or only suppressing symptoms. It's your responsibility to proactively gain an understanding of your health challenges, not the doctor's sole responsibility to teach you. Learn what it takes to keep your body healthy.

We need doctors, especially for critical care situations such as falls, auto accidents, and broken bones. However, the body does the healing, not the doctor. Doctors set us on a path to healing. The body heals based on the quality of care it receives.

Taking 100% Responsibility

The majority of people delegate the responsibility for their health to healthcare professionals. They do whatever a counselor or doctor says without question because the professionals are the ones that went to school for it, right? They know more about how the human body works than most of us, but you know your body better than they do. You live in your body.

I follow Dr. Suneel Dhand on social media that helps me to know and understand the medical system here in the United States. He is a licensed physician specializing in internal and lifestyle medicine. He teaches how to beat the system that makes you sick.

Most doctors have good intentions but the medical industry is ultimately a business. Like any business, it is always looking for more business. Doctors are there to assist you, but make sure you work *with* a doctor; don't just delegate your responsibility to improve your health. Treatments create more business, cures don't. Do your own research. It is okay to question your doctor to gain knowledge about your situation.

You can also ask your intuition what is right for you. Your infinite self knows. Medication and supplements should lead you to healing, not a way of life. The goal is to heal and be off all medication if possible.

The Pervasiveness of Medication

Research indicates that as much as 70% of all people in the United States are on some type of medication. It is clearly disclosed there are many side effects. Putting anything in your body that tries to overrule your natural homeostasis can limit your balance thus affecting your connectivity to your mind and spirit. There is so much quality information available today regarding health. Educate yourself so you can take more control of your health. That is awareness.

The Goal is to Feel Good

When we are young, most of us who work out do it to make ourselves look good. As we age, most work out to improve their health and to feel good. We still want to look good, but health becomes the priority later in life. Whatever your age, love yourself by making physical health your priority. Looking good is the natural beneficial byproduct of taking care of yourself, not the priority. Understand the meaningful reasons we need to exercise and eat right.

Body Acceptance

Your body has different sizes and shapes throughout your life, but it's the perfect you. What you do with that body creates your reality.

When you resist your body, you resist life, and you become imbalanced. Your body is your friend, not your enemy, but it feels that way when you see it as flawed and not what you "want."

No one can deny their body and love themselves. Love your body unconditionally, while understanding your health, then your body will love and take care of you.

Accept the Earth's Healing

The Earth naturally heals itself. To prove it, clear an area of all vegetation. Soon after, the ground will begin to sprout new vegetation and within a few years, it will be like it was never cleared. That is the Earth naturally healing itself.

As we previously discussed, your body is the same - it will naturally heal. Did you know the Earth can help your body heal? Your body can absorb the Earth's energy, which assists your body towards homeostasis. It is a natural way of healing called "earthing," also known as "grounding."

We ground when we walk on grass, work in the garden, play on the beach, or otherwise physically connect with the Earth. The healing energy comes from the Earth's life force. The Earth even has a heartbeat called the Schumann resonance.

Today's typical lifestyle limits our access to this benefit because we are usually insulated from the Earth's soil by our shoes, homes, and cars.

Dr. Laura Koniver, MD has demonstrated that grounding improves nutrition, hydration, air quality, and sleep. Being grounded is the foundation of body balance. It is your benchmark.

Furthermore, Dr. Stephen T. Sinatra, MD discusses in his book "Earthing" how the Earth can neutralize free radicals. Your connection to the Earth is one of the best antioxidants and anti-inflammatories and it costs you nothing. I ground myself daily.

Many love to go hiking, work in the garden, or do other outside activities. It is something within that creates that desire to get outside. It is your body seeking that healing energy. It is your intuition guiding you to homeostasis.

Feeling a little off? Begin grounding daily and see if you start to feel more balanced in mind, body, and spirit.

I Walk the Walk

After a childhood of trauma and struggles, during my healing period, I realized that my body was off balance when I suddenly began to unnaturally gain weight. It was a lesson, my body yelling at me saying, "I need some attention!"

My adrenals and other functions were far out of balance. I now work with doctors that specialize in functional medicine, which focuses on getting patients balanced and then maintaining health rather than treating or managing illness.

I am pleased to say, at almost 60 years of age, that I am on no medication at the time of this writing. After years of numbing the pains of trauma with alcohol, I am now free of the desire to numb. I am working on a daily body health routine. The healthier my body, the stronger my intuition, and the stronger my immune system.

I contribute to my body's health not only through physical exercise, but in attitude, gratitude, and appreciation of my life. I thank my body every day for taking care of me and supporting me in accomplishing my goals.

Summary of Body Health

I noticed that when I did not have self-love I would drink and self-sabotage. When I was living in harmony I was balanced, worked out, ate right, and treated myself with respect and love.

The more critical you are of your body, the more out of balance you will be in mind and spirit. When you take care of your body, your body will in turn take care of your mind and spirit. You can't neglect one without neglecting the other two.

When you are in total balance, you are in homeostasis and you feel good. You think positive thoughts and you feel gratitude and a desire to do good to all those around you. You attract amazing things in your life.

Understand your body and its purpose. Be kind to your body and your body will be kind to you.

Take care of your body.
It's the only one you have.

Joe Cox, Jr.

CHAPTER 8

Wholeness of the Spirit

Wholeness = (*Mind Balance* + Body Balance + **Spirit Balance**)

In this chapter, we will discuss your spirit and how it plays a role in your happiness. Without spirit balance, it is impossible to achieve authentic happiness. The spirit is the foundation of wholeness. The goal is to attain wholeness to attract richness and happiness to experience your heaven here on Earth.

Mind and body health are directly affected by your spirit. We are all infinite beings having a physical experience. It is often said, "Life is so tough that no one makes it out alive." While it is true that life can be tough, it is much tougher if you do not understand the rules that guide your life. Clarity is understanding how to live a physical life, following the unseen laws, guided by your intuition, to result in attracting happiness in all you do.

Understanding More About Yourself

Have you noticed that almost all of us ask the question, "What is my purpose?" If we are all asking that same question, there must be a deeper purpose built into humanity as a whole.

Why was I born? What is my purpose? What is the meaning of it all? When a person begins to ask these questions, they are in the first stage of their personal growth. This is the first stage of authentic maturity.

True Maturity

Most people consider age to be the signifier of when a person changes from being a child, to an adolescent, and then to an adult. Some would say achievements like graduation or moving out of their childhood homes are more significant, but that would be thinking from the ego.

The official moment a person arrives at adulthood has nothing to do with the outside world. It is the moment that a person begins to seek themselves. It is the moment that one begins to consider the spiritual nature of humanity. A 16-year-old adult could be seen as an "old soul", while an enabled 40-year-old child is living in his parents' basement. It all depends on the control and understanding of the real you, the you within, not just the flesh.

Perfect Order

You are the perfect you. You are not broken and you don't need to be fixed, nor does anybody else. We all live in an unseen world of perfect order. Violating that perfect order, knowingly or unknowingly, creates chaos in our lives.

To understand why bad things happen to good people we must understand the laws that regulate our lives here on Earth. If you feel you are a good person but you are living a life of chaos, chances are you're not living in flow with natural law. You're not following the laws that apply to your life. Most would follow these laws if they were aware of them.

It's like driving down the street and being pulled over and getting a ticket for a law that you broke that you didn't know existed. You still have to pay the fine. Ignorance of the law is irrelevant. Life is the same way. In life, when we break natural laws that we don't understand, we are still required to pay the fine with pain and suffering until we learn and follow the laws.

The law of gravity is an example of one such law that we cannot see but it exists. If a righteous guy and a criminal both fall from the same cliff, does one or the other have a better chance of surviving? That law of physics apply to both of them equally. Righteousness does not sway the law of gravity. Both men will face a similar outcome relative to the fall.

Gravity is just one example of these natural laws. There are many others. I lived for years not knowing these other natural laws existed. In turn, my life was like a rollercoaster, up and down. I was out of balance until I began to understand the elements of my life that were out of harmony with life laws and the reasons behind that misalignment. Once I gained that knowledge, my life took an incredible turn for the better.

When I lived in accordance with these natural laws, suffering and struggling slowly ceased. Fight against or ignore these laws by living a life controlled by emotions and ego, and you will create your own hell, and your suffering and struggle will continue. Only through awareness will you see and understand the answers through wisdom. Only through living in truth will you gain awareness of these answers hidden in plain sight. Awareness in all things welcomes enlightenment, where all meaningful answers are found.

Becoming Enlightened

Enlightenment or to be enlightened is nothing more than having greater wisdom and understanding of your being by connecting to your source within, also known as your higher power or your infinite self. Most people make life far more complicated than it needs to be. Confusion will do that, but clarity simplifies life.

There are common life laws that govern your daily experience here on Earth. Understanding and following these natural laws grants you the ability to experience, learn, and gain abundance in all things. When living by these laws you come to understand how life works *for* you to give you the abundance you desire.

To attain authentic happiness is a virtue. It is your duty to seek and follow the rules of life to welcome happiness. You are the only thing in the way of your happiness. Happiness is not the purpose of life, but it is the reward for a life well lived.

Live in Harmony with Life

Harmony is being in perfect accord with goodness, beauty, and your higher power. It comes when one is living in flow with life, controlling only oneself, and allowing others to walk their own paths. Everyone moves at their own pace and has their own path. Allow each to walk that path without your interference.

Following the laws for balance in wholeness allows you to live in harmony. Living a harmonious life attracts happiness.

> *Peace is the spirit letting you know that you are living a life in harmony with your higher self.*
>
> *Joe Cox, Jr.*

Live your life in harmony with these natural laws, then you will overcome your challenges. Your life will be in flow and wholeness will be yours.

Spirituality

Spirituality is about your individual connection to your intuition, higher power, and authentic self. Many books have been written about how to live our lives. Each book has very different interpretations and arguments about who is right and who is wrong. With spiritual laws, there is no right or wrong, there is only truth, one truth, and it is in perfect order. Spiritual laws removes the confusion and gives clarity. Each person has their own path. In finding yourself, you heal yourself. When you heal yourself, you will heal the world.

Tolerance of Others

Tolerance is a virtue. It works in harmony with spirituality. Tolerance is defined as the ability to accept something outside yourself that you know is out of order with truth while standing in peace within yourself. Tolerance is choosing not to force your opinion on another. It is about controlling ourselves without the desire to control others, thus allowing each to live the life they desire without our interference.

The most common violation we make of this law is attempting to control others by trying to change or rescue them. This mistake is made in many marriages and other intimate relationships. We are sure to be disappointed because controlling others breaks natural law. When we try to assert control over others, we interfere with their life paths and ignore our own path. We are bound by these laws whether we accept them or not. They are a part of us. Accept and live by these laws and you will thrive.

Peace is the heartbeat of happiness.

Joe Cox, Jr.

Suffering is Optional

Many believe life is suffering. I find that life can be painful at times, but suffering is optional. Suffering comes from ignorance and failure to live by natural law. Most of my life has been suffering because I didn't understand life laws. If I'd had this information at age 16, my suffering would have been drastically reduced and my life quality would have increased my joy and happiness.

Since I began practicing living these natural laws, I went from suicidal depression to thriving with abundance in all areas of my life including making more money than ever before and attracting and marrying my soulmate. It's all about the lesson and understanding how to process life experiences.

Rules to the Game of Life

Imagine you're playing a game called "The Game of Life." It has rules which regulate and affect your everyday life and must be followed in order to win. Understanding and playing by these rules will change your life for the better in miraculous ways.

You may recognize some of the rules, while others are new to you. These laws will help give you clarity when you ask, "Why did this happen to me?" Look for the lesson. These rules are your guardrails for life. They will help guide you.

1. ***Rule of Oneness:*** Humans are all interconnected through collective consciousness. This is a foundational rule and applies to all others. Put simply, when you help others, you are helping yourself. When you hurt another, you are hurting yourself. We grow through our connections to each other, as we offer guidance to one another while allowing others to walk their own path. Lesson: When you get your own life in order, you have done your part to fix the world through collective consciousness.

2. _Rule of Attraction_: We attract what we are, not what we want. Think positive, attract positive. To manifest the things you desire in your life, take the steps needed:

   a. _Decide_ what you desire, in mind, body, and spirit.

   b. _Ask_ the universe in detail (color, size, location, etc.)

   c. _Visualize_ it with increasing detail.

   d. _Feel_ it; taste it; smell it; hold it in your mind and gut like it is already there.

   e. Give _gratitude_ for receiving it, even before you actually receive it.

   f. _Trust, believe, and have faith in the capacity of your higher power to deliver what you desire. You are now open to receiving it. It is as if you have already received it._

   g. _Take action_ to facilitate receiving it. Faith without works is dead. Be pure in your intent and desires.

   Lesson: You attract everything in your life through the intent of your thoughts, desires, and actions.

3. _Rule of Cause and Effect_: Some call it consequences. It is the phenomena of action and intention causing one another. If someone steals from another, eventually something will be stolen from them in return. Lesson: No one ever really gets away with anything. Things always come back around, just not necessarily in your desired timeframe.

4. _Rule of Words:_ Words are powerful. Every word builds or destroys. Words either bless or curse. Think before you speak. Only speak words that benefit you and all those around you. Lesson: Only use words you want for yourself. Positive and beneficial words manifest beautiful futures.

5. _Rule of Maturity:_ Babies are born pure, with no pre-conceived notions or prejudices. They communicate with emotions, as designed. When you were a child, you behaved as a child. You did childish things. When you became an adult, you put away those childish things. Maturity thrives on personal growth. It begins with a desire for adult intelligence and always seeks wisdom through a connection with your higher, spirit self. With maturity comes self-awareness and self-control. We are each 100% accountable and responsible for our own actions. Live your life with genuine intent, always trying to do your best. Lesson: Many adults live childishly, prioritizing entertainment and distractions. It's your job to learn the lessons of life, not anyone's job to teach you. You must be mature enough to seek the answers needed for wholeness, richness, and happiness.

6. _Rule of Warning:_ Nothing happens in life without previous notice. Put your life in order. Failure to heed warnings and prepare invites suffering. Following this rule will limit unnecessary pain and suffering. A well-prepared person has no need to fear life. Lesson: Be prepared in all you do. Heed your warnings. Seek awareness. Proactively prepare for all possibilities in life.

7. _Rule of Opportunity:_ Life offers unlimited opportunities. Learn to seek and recognize them. They are always around you. Awareness is seeing things that others don't. It's your job to seek it, not another's to lead you to it. Lesson: Opportunity is often disguised as work and leads to meaning, purpose, and abundance.

8. _Rule of Inquiry:_ Don't assume anything. Inquire, question, and seek truth in all you do. Intuition will increase your capacity to recognize your path. Think, ponder, and meditate. With effort, you will receive your clear answer. You will see, feel, and/or know the answer because of your awareness. Lesson: Question everything and seek truth. Your intuition will confirm.

9. _Rule of Three:_ Know the difference between perseverance and stubbornness. Things that are meant to be, will flow into place naturally. Things that are not will fall apart. Try a maximum of three times to fix an issue. You should not have to force it. Look for signs of whether or not you are on a blessed path. Stubbornness is ignoring your intuition and forcing a round object through a proverbial square hole. Lesson: Learn when to persevere and when to make a change. Stubbornness only adds to pain and suffering. Results happen with perseverance when on the proper path.

10. _Rule of Perpetual Transmutation of Energy:_ Your energy is your fuel for life. This rule governs the management of that energy. Sometimes we give and sometimes we receive. Positive connections leave you with energy left over at the end of the day. Toxic people will drain you of your joy. Stay aware of who you let into your circle. Avoid energy "vampires." No one has a right to your energy unless you allow it. Your source is always there to help you recharge. Lesson: Protect your energy. Each person will build you up or drain you. Your higher power has unlimited capacity to replenish your energy.

11. _Rule of Saturation:_ The saturation point is the point in one's life when that person makes a change. Suffering is required for transcendence, but the length of time spent suffering is up to us. This is the moment when you are ready to accept your lesson and progress to the next level toward wholeness. Be open to inner change; accept life as it is, even the things you cannot change. Lesson: Progress from lessons toward greater wholeness through acceptance.

12. _Rule of Generation:_ We are each born into unique circumstances, but our paths are our own creations. You design your life through your thoughts, feelings, beliefs, and actions one decision at a time. Lesson: We have no control over the various circumstances we were born into, but once we are on our own, our lives are our own creations.

13. _Rule of Compensation:_ This is a rule regarding the balance of give and take. Balance will eventually be established in all things. Actions and services entitle us to compensation. This law refers to the natural state of win-win situations. It is commerce in harmony. This law also applies to relationships. Trust returns trust when a relationship is in a harmonious state. Giving without receiving causes an imbalance and eventually exhausts resources. Receiving without giving produces poverty. Each person must offer a service to others in order to be in balance. Don't just give a man a fish; teach him how to fish. Idleness drains resources and does not honor one's responsibility of service to others. Lesson: Idleness destroys. It is your duty to contribute to society. You are entitled to be compensated for your contribution, either monetarily or in spirit.

14. _Rule of Empty Spaces_: Nature despises a vacuum and tends to fill the space. If we don't proactively and intentionally fill our lives, our lives will randomly be filled. Fill your life with productive intent. Lesson: Live intentionally. You become what you think and feel. Your future is filled and created by your thoughts and actions.

15. _Rule of Option for Love_: First is self-love, then comes attracting love. You cannot give what you do not have for yourself. Many people in intimate relationships violate this rule by doing the opposite - neglecting self-love and defining their worth according to someone else's willingness or ability to accept them. Love, compassion, and acceptance are the foundation and inspiration of the spirit. Love has no wants. Lesson: Love is given unconditionally. First, seek self-love, then seek to be loved. Seek to share love with others, not to depend on receiving love from others. Love starts from within, not from without.

16. _Rule of Mirroring_: This rule indicates that the qualities you notice in others are a reflection of yourself. You will see in others your strengths and your faults. Lesson: Judging others is self-sabotage. Judging others is judging ourselves. How you see others says nothing about them but everything about you.

17. _Rule of Understanding:_ This rule indicates that if you haven't learned the intended lesson from an experience then you will continue to have similar experiences until the lesson is learned. A person who says, "This happens to me all the time" does so because a lesson must be learned before one can proceed to the next level of growth. Seek the wisdom in each lesson. Lesson: Challenges do not indicate that you are being punished, but simply that you haven't yet learned an important life lesson. There is a reason the same things keep happening, or why you keep attracting the same unhealthy relationships. Life happens _for_ you, not _to_ you. Understanding your lesson will set you free.

18. _Rule of Self-Preservation:_ We are designed to first survive, then thrive. Everyone has a life force, that spark for life given at birth. The higher one's consciousness, the stronger one's life force, and the greater one's capacity for self-preservation. Unregulated thoughts, emotions, and feelings can lower your life force and destroy you from within. Lesson: You are born with a strong life force. Life wants you to thrive. Self-love and connection to your inner source strengthen this force. Every act in life increases or lowers your inner life force. Never, Ever Give Up!

Summary of the Rules

Apply these rules and living life well will become much simpler. Living a life of integrity, character, and honor come from following these rules. If your life is complicated and difficult, it's only because you are not following the rules. There are other rules, but these are the most important for our lives today. Following these rules puts you in harmony with your inner and outer world. Following these rules will reduce your stress, your worry, and any concerns that are outside of your control. The universal rules are in control and you will be guided if you allow them.

> *Happiness is not the purpose of life,*
> *but seeking meaning and purpose in life*
> *attracts happiness everywhere you go*
>
> *Joe Cox, Jr.*

It is believed that "sin" is a religious thing. It's a humanity thing. Whether from Greek or Hebrew, it means to "miss the mark." It is to miss the mark of whatever we are aiming at. We first must understand and have clarity of the proper target.

The overall purpose of life is to grow and develop your infinite self through a physical experience. You are to live life to the fullest. Live, learn, and become a master of self.

Spend your time wisely. Too many folks waste time on un-beneficial things. We all need play and relaxation as part of our balance in all things. Maturity is doing your work first before being entertained. By playing by the rules of the game of life, everyone wins.

CHAPTER 9

The Power of Forgiveness

What would you say if I told you that it's in your best interest to forgive everybody who has ever hurt you?

Forgive them? So, now you're telling me to forgive the jerks? Am I just supposed to take it and let them get away with what they have done? No way! If I forgive them, they win. Right? Then they will just do it again.

That is the way many people believe forgiveness works. Someone wins, someone loses. Many resist even considering forgiveness. Understand that forgiveness is not a religious thing. It is a humanity thing. It is a consciousness thing. If you want to live an amazing life, skipping forgiveness is not an option. Your spirit body requires forgiveness for wholeness. Without forgiveness, you carry toxic emotions within and those are manifested through the body with illness and sickness. Without learning to forgive, you are guaranteed to stay stuck with a low consciousness. There are no winners without forgiveness. We will examine in this chapter how forgiveness can become possible for anyone.

Many believe that if someone made them feel like a fool and that someone isn't punished, then that person will continue the same behavior. It is our duty to punish them, right? Our conscious minds believe we are the ones responsible to make sure they are punished. It's an ego thing. I get it. I have been there. I said the same thing for years and I kept struggling. The goal is to rid yourself of the toxic energy behind the offense. What if I told you the *best way to get even* is to forgive? Follow me here for a minute...

Let me explain what I mean by forgiveness. Forgiving others for their offenses against you is for your benefit. Forgiving does not mean the offender gets away with anything. No one ever gets away with anything in the long run. Natural laws will not allow it. Forgiveness is not releasing that person from the responsibility or accountability for what was done. You are forgiving for *your* sake. Withholding forgiveness is self-defeating and you will lose every time. The purpose of forgiveness is to release the toxic energies behind the offense thus releasing you from its harmful influence.

As long as you hold on to the toxic energy of hurt and betrayal, it will eat you alive from the inside out. It will affect every aspect of your life whether you realize it or not. Forgiveness empowers and returns control to you. Forgiveness increases your consciousness thus increasing your connection with your higher power.

Let's say the person that injured you dies. Do you automatically forgive or do you still hold on to those feelings against them? Do you still feel anger toward a dead person? If so, you are allowing them to control you from the grave. How is that possible? Because it's about you, not about them. It's all about how you *react* to the offense that matters in the game of life.

When you don't forgive, your pain can swell into bitterness, vindictiveness, anger, and other negative emotions. It's like an acid that eats through your spirit. Forgiveness is imperative for wholeness which leads you to happiness. Based on my findings through observing, talking to, and teaching people over the last 40 years, forgiveness is possibly the number one obstacle in people's lives, keeping them in misery, in lack, stuck, and unable to move forward into prosperity, thus keeping them from happiness.

Who Wins?

Why does it have to be a somebody wins, somebody loses situation? The ego believes someone has to win in a toxic situation. The truth is that without forgiveness, both people involved will lose.

The good news is that no one is allowed to get away with anything. Ever! They can't. Accountability is one of the laws of nature. My life is a testament to that. When you forgive, set boundaries, and release toxic energy by letting it go, just stand back and watch what happens over time. I have lived long enough to see these scenarios play out. Many times it's taken years but everything in life plays out according to everyone's choices.

Forgiving is a self-care play in the game of life. It is really just about you, not those who have hurt you. You don't need their participation to forgive them. They created a toxic situation for you. With forgiveness, you choose to eliminate the toxicity in your space.

Letting hurt go allows you to prevail in life. Cause and effect will come to visit others and balance all things in nature, maybe not on your schedule, but it will always happen at just the right time. You may never see it happen, but it will.

Getting Even

Forgiveness benefits you in every way, but your conscious mind, your ego, may not see it that way. The ego will tell you to be defensive, to engage your fight or flight mode. It wants you to use your auto-response to strike back. The problem with this approach is that it only creates more toxic energy. We were designed with the "fight or flight" instinct to respond effectively to physical threats. Understanding and forgiving release the spirit from emotional threats. It's not your job to correct or hold on to the psychological and emotional pain inflicted on you by others.

If you attempt to "even the score" and pass judgment on the offender in your own court for what they have done, you in turn accept their toxic energy. You have interfered with one of their lessons in life and you have failed to learn your lesson. In passing judgment and seeking to balance the scales, you voluntarily accept additional pain and suffering.

Just look around at all the angry people in the world. Most of them are carrying resentment, bitterness, envy, jealousy, and vindictiveness. These emotions and feelings lower their consciousness levels, taking away their peace and harmony, and destroying their ability to connect to their higher selves. As they blame everybody else for their problems, they are blinded to the reality of their own potential greatness.

It's About the Lesson

Do you want to stop being betrayed? This is how.

Have you ever heard someone who was upset say "This always happens to me." Bingo! You just heard that person confess that they didn't learn their lesson the last time it happened to them. People in harmony who are balanced in wholeness will never say that about anything.

Another very common evidence of someone missing a life lesson is when people continually make poor dating choices. They attract what they are, not what they want. The lesson is to work on yourself first. Become the person you want to attract, then you will attract the person that is the right fit for you. Too many people go around thinking others are going to fix their problems while still hanging on to anger from a past relationship. Then they attract people who they think need fixing. It's simple to correct when you understand how it works. Fix yourself and then you will attract people who don't need to be fixed. The easiest way forward is to forgive all.

If you are holding on to the angry energy of past relation-ships, you will attract the same energy that you despise in another person because you have not yet come to a healthy resolution for your previous relationship. Make sense yet?

Without learning the lessons of forgiveness, we set ourselves up for failure because we are stuck holding on to old, negative energy, refusing to open up to the truth. Forgiveness will set you free.

An Eye Opener

Want to attract your authentic and genuine love? Want the right person for you? Forgiveness will create the environment for you to attract the most beneficial relationships into your life.

You have heard, "like attracts like", and also "opposites attract." Which one is right? They are both right but let's look at what is typically happening in each circumstance.

When "like attracts like," you are attracted to someone on a similar consciousness level as you. You attract what you are, not necessarily what you want. This is the level at which you and the other person are each connected to your respective sources, higher power, internal guidance systems, and intuitions. You're both headed in the same direction in life.

When "opposites attract," you are attracting a person that complements you. They have strengths where you have weaknesses and vice versa, like Yin and Yang. Masculine and feminine energies normally do this, attracting the opposites like a magnet. This is natural law seeking balance in a union of two. This is often a beneficial connection because opposite energies can balance out each other.

To attract the "right" person, it is in your best interest to attract someone with both qualities, one that complements your attributes and is on the same consciousness level as you. Such an attraction offers balance in different aspects of life, which creates wholeness. Being in a relationship, you can't attract happiness without balance in both areas. Each type of attraction has two people in balance with one another. This applies to friends and a mate for life. The purpose is for each one to help the other develop themselves in this life.

Your goal is to attract people in your life with qualities that complement yours but who have the same consciousness and spiritual level so you can walk together on the path of life.

Please note that most relationships we enter into right after a breakup are some type of rebound relationship, created out of fear, usually the fear of being alone. In that situation, you would attract other people who live in fear. A great example is someone with low self-worth attracting someone with self-sabotaging behavior. These two people would be at a similar consciousness level, possibly in a narcissistic, code-pendent relationship. They are a mirror of one another's lack of self-worth and self-love. Simply put, dysfunctional people often unconsciously attract other dysfunctional people, each trying to fix the other rather than simply fixing themselves.

Time to Change

If you are making harmful choices through poor habits you will continue down an unbeneficial path. You will continue to struggle until you have had enough pain and suffering to change your direction.

Have you ever heard someone say, in a loud and frustrated voice, "I HAVE HAD ENOUGH?" That is a good sign. It's a sign that change is about to happen. Many choose just to complain about their struggles and continue the same dysfunctional behavior pattern that leads to a life of suffering. You will never have more pain than you are willing to tolerate.

> **You will never have more of anything in life than what you are willing to tolerate.**
>
> *Joe Cox, Jr.*

If you tolerate abuse, then that is what you will have. Life does not test you, but it will keep guiding you with lessons to help you find your balance. Where and how you live your emotional life is determined by your own chosen tolerance level.

Everyone chooses to live life somewhere along the spectrum between love and chaos. Your tolerance level determines where on that spectrum you reside. With no tolerance for dysfunction, and with forgiveness, life will push you toward the love and harmony end of the spectrum.

Every event happens by design *for you,* not *to you.* A betrayal is simply a lesson. The lesson is that a particular person can't be trusted, so you need to set healthy boundaries and, if necessary, get them out of your life, then release the emotional pain by letting it go. Forgiving someone does that, while holding on to resentment keeps their toxicity in your life and keeps your consciousness level down.

Pain, frustration, depression, anxiety, and many other feelings and emotions are lessons provided to teach us, not to punish us. We punish ourselves by not learning the lesson. As soon as you understand the lesson, you can heal everything within. Each emotion sends us signals. Pain lets us know we have a problem that should not be ignored. It's to get our attention. It tells us we need to make a change. It's simply telling you, "Don't do that again."

It reminds me of an old saying, "To find out if you really have a friend, loan them some money." If you never see them again, you did yourself a favor. You learned your lesson. Forgive them, forget the money, and the problem is gone. The money will come back to you eventually tenfold.

We Become What We Feel

When people choose not to forgive and instead obsess over how they were wronged, they begin to hate the person who wronged them, and the more their hatred builds, the more they become like the person they perceive has wronged them. In other words, you become the very thing that you hate most. This is one of the strange hidden lessons in life. That alone seems to be a good enough reason to forgive. You cannot have love for yourself while holding on to hate.

Many people did horrible things to me. My anger and thoughts of vengeance were like a bag of rocks I carried on my back everywhere I went. After years of holding onto anger and bitterness, I came to understand the principles behind forgiveness. Once I learned where those emotions were located within me and saw how they were controlling me and that I was allowing it, it was easier to see that letting it all go was the right choice once I had understanding in my heart. Actually letting it go, however, was a little more difficult.

It took practice to change my thought patterns about the pain I had been through. It was a simple process but not always an easy one. As I went through the process of forgiveness, I began to like myself, then began to accept love within. I gained the self-love I had never had before.

I struggled for many years until I learned to open my spiritual eyes and see the lessons. I considered the whole experience from the outside looking in.

My problem was that I kept thinking of myself as a victim. Victims don't have control. People who identify as victims don't learn the life lessons associated with their experiences. They get comfortable in victimhood. They assume that carrying pain is a requirement of life. It's not! This assumption is only true if you don't understand how to change by taking control of your life. It's your decision.

Another reason to let go of toxic energy is that toxic people age much faster than forgiving people. Again, look around. People who smile every day look prettier and age more gracefully. They feel better and have more positive energy. That might be the best reason to forgive.

Narcissists and Abusers

We have talked about forgiveness for smaller offenses like lying and not paying back borrowed money, but what about heavy, life-changing damage that some people inflict on others? What about people who seem to get joy from hurting others? It's especially painful to be abused or betrayed by a family member. That is a trauma that cuts deep within the spirit. If you have had this happen to you, you understand what I am talking about.

Mothers, fathers, siblings, husbands, wives, and adult children - we instinctively trust these relationships, so it hurts worse when they betray us. That loss of trust and connection breaks us. It's not as easy to move on when the offender is family. How do you move on from that?

Most of these types of betrayals have previous abusive intentions and behaviors attached to them. Someone betrayed that person, so they paid it forward. In other words, it was not an accident. They knew what they were doing. They chose to stay in the ego and failed to learn their past lesson. You cannot help them understand. Let them walk their own path. It's not up to you to fix them. Just heal yourself.

Abusive behaviors are the result of people being dominated by their egos. They are disconnected from self. They are very low-energy people who lack any connection to their source, thus they live by the laws created by the ego, believing someone must lose for them to win. We can only understand behaviors relative to our consciousness level. If you don't understand it, that means you have risen above it. It's not healthy to dwell on it. Forgive and move on.

In their minds, they won. In our minds, they lost everything that mattered.

Releasing Life's Burdens

Toxic energy is often created by a situation you did not knowingly instigate or welcome. Imagine a big ball of toxic energy being created through a negative situation. You have a choice. You can hold on to that energy or you can give it back. If you forgive, you are returning the toxic energy to whoever passed it on to you. If you engage with it, you accept it and carry it with you. The more people that engage with it or the more you dwell on it, the bigger it gets.

Whoever creates the toxic energy is required to carry it unless you *choose* to carry it. You choose to carry it when you don't forgive but instead choose bitterness and anger. Forgiveness is about releasing any negative energy around a situation that burdens you with extra mental or emotional baggage. This release of toxic energy is your rejection of their drama and toxic behavior.

Picture yourself gathering up all the toxic energy from past abuse and betrayal and forming it into a big ball. Now see yourself handing it back to the offenders. Then, brush off your hands, turn around, and walk the other way. Visualize it like it's really happening in front of you because, in the spiritual realm, it did happen. Now that you have imagined yourself releasing all of that toxic energy and returning it, don't you feel better?

Once offenders have their toxic energy back, they can't get rid of it until they make peace with their source. It is now between them and their creator. Let it go and let natural law settle the score, not you. That's not your job. Your job is growth.

The only way to completely eliminate toxic energy is through giving and receiving forgiveness and making things right with one another.

Say you release toxic energy through forgiveness without the offender's participation, and then later they come to ask for your forgiveness. If you fail to accept their apology, or if you refuse to accept someone else's forgiveness, then you never truly forgave. Guess who is going to carry the negativity? You!

Let Trust Be Earned

Why do we trust? Because trust builds connections. We instinctively seek out authentic connections based on trust and vulnerability. Love requires it. People who go through life not trusting anyone typically feel disconnected. The greatest meaning in life includes that connection.

To protect yourself, never give your trust freely. Make sure your trust is earned. Meaning, the more someone must work for your trust, the less likely they are to breach it. Trust too fast, then they have little invested in you, and they may feel they have nothing to lose by betraying your trust. Before you give your trust, make sure others have time and energy invested in that trust. Investment creates value.

Setting Boundaries

Forgiving someone does not require that you allow them to still have a place in your life. Forgiveness means releasing a person's negative energy from within yourself and sending it back to them. You then have every right to set a boundary you are comfortable with even if that means keeping them completely out of your life. If they ask your forgiveness and make amends, you can then reassess your boundaries. Look to your intuition for guidance here.

Red Flags

Let's look at the lesson that Earth School is trying to teach us. When a person's negative intentions drain your energy, it is time to put up a boundary. After you forgive, you set boundaries to protect yourself. If an offender tries to guilt you or manipulate you over your set boundaries, that is just a "red flag" that you must uphold those boundaries to protect yourself.

A red flag is a sign that a toxic behavior is headed toward you so if you don't have clear boundaries, now is the time to protect yourself. Too many times I saw the red flags and did not protect myself. Look for red flags with everyone in your life. Make protecting yourself a priority.

Don't Get Stuck

When you're stuck, it simply means you have stopped moving forward. Being stuck means you are confused about something and need clarity. Since time always moves forward, if you're stuck, you're not growing. The answer you need is out there, so go looking for it, especially in books. I have found my most impactful answers in books. Reading also provides alone time to think and meditate. After you've read something that resonates with you, check with your intuition to determine if it is true. Most of the time, forgiveness is needed to get unstuck.

People Change

I have heard "people can change" and also that "people never change". From all my years of living, this is what I have found:

People can change, and a few do, but the very large majority don't. People have a core being. They live that core unless they decide to take a different path. They walk the path that they choose. The ones who change are strong people who desire to improve. They want to be their best selves and gain awareness. Allow people the opportunity to change but remember that it's not your job to lower your standards or boundaries for someone else's growth. Lowering your standards for another is betraying yourself.

Birth of Wisdom

All emotions are energy. If someone betrays you, you may feel sick to your stomach or angry. That is your internal guidance system warning you not to trust that person again. So ask yourself, *What is the lesson I need to learn so this will not happen again?*

Remember this when it comes to forgiveness and the lesson: The event of abuse is painful. Remembering the event without forgiveness is suffering. However, *your memory of the event without emotion is forgiveness, and with forgiveness comes wisdom.* This is how wisdom is born. Forgiveness and wisdom work hand in hand. Yes, it happened to you once, but never again. Lesson learned - you now have the wisdom to protect yourself and others around you.

Forgiving others is your choice and your power. Forgiving is a process and takes time. It is finding the resolve to welcome peace for yourself. After I forgave those in my family who hurt me, the unseen doors of prosperity and abundance could open. My intention of letting go allowed me to take control of my own life.

Great things happen when we forgive. It's not easy in the beginning. It took time to accept these natural laws into my belief system, but I learned my lesson. Now no one can betray me unless I allow myself to be vulnerable to them. I now have boundaries. So, be careful who you trust. Respect is given unconditionally, but trust should always be earned over time.

Sure Forgiveness

How do you know when you have forgiven someone? The first sign is that you don't think about or analyze what happened anymore. Another way is you have converted your anger and bitterness toward them into sadness for them, realizing in truth, they betrayed themselves as much as they betrayed you.

Summary

Remember, I am the one that not even a mother could love. So, how did I ever forgive my mother? I recognized that her inability to love me had nothing to do with me. It had everything to do with her own lack of self-love. I don't feel bitterness towards her anymore. I feel only sadness for her. She failed to learn her lesson in life. I maintain healthy boundaries and I bless her on her path.

Memory of the event without emotion is forgiveness, and with forgiveness comes wisdom.

Joe Cox, Jr.

CHAPTER 10

Living a Life of Richness

Happiness = Wholeness (Within) + **Richness (Outside of You)**

Richness is the final variable in our equation for happiness. Wealth is often misconstrued as richness, but they are not the same.

Wealth is the focus on and attainment of money and tangible possessions. *Richness* is far more vast. It is a state of plenty and abundance in all things, prosperity, including money, but not limited to monetary wealth. You could also refer to it as "life richness".

Balance in richness means being well-rounded and having pleasure, fun, joy, and quality experiences. It includes learning, travel, relationships, family, accomplishments, and all your connections to anything outside of you while on this earthly plain.

We are designed to live in wholeness, and when we do, all things are open to us in richness. Once we become whole and we are in balance, our inner wholeness can easily manifest to lead us to the level of wealth, prosperity, and abundance that we seek. In return, we attract happiness in all we do.

Richness Required

Since we have physical bodies in a physical world, we can't ignore them. We must address the impact our choices have on our mortal bodies. The external world affects our inner world in all aspects: mind, body, and spirit. The common question is, if we can attain happiness and wholeness, why do we need richness to remain in a state of happiness? Why do we need prosperity and abundance?

If you have reached the state of happiness, that means you already have attained some level of richness. I don't believe you can attain a state of happiness in this mortal world without some level of richness. However, the level of richness is your choice.

There is no benefit to ignore your external, mortal existence by only working on your inner spiritual self and ignoring your outer world. It's about balance. Both aspects of our life experience must work together to form happiness. Working on our wholeness in relation to our external experience attracts happiness.

Knowing how to balance the material world with our inner world has confused many through the years. Since we are spiritual beings, we need to understand where and how material things fit into our lives and how happiness is attained while we are here on Earth. When do material things become a detriment versus a blessing?

Gaining and maintaining happiness is relatively simple if you have all the necessary components. Our goal is to be able to see the whole picture. Addressing material things is challenging for many people seeking spirituality. They struggle to gain clarity regarding the right approach to material things. Once we understand, it is simple to make the decisions that open the world of prosperity to us.

It's not that material things are evil; they are healthy for us when properly utilized. The harm is not in possessing the items. It's *how* the items are obtained and used that creates the good or bad, right or wrong.

Attachment

A detrimental attachment is when a person experiences an attachment to a physical object. It's when we find security in material items rather than from within. A physical attachment is detrimental to your balance and wellbeing. Why? Because everything material is temporary. Wholeness is infinite and is attached to nothing temporary. You can only experience a sense of loss if you are attached to a temporary item.

The ego prefers physical attachments. To be attached to an item is to identify with that item. When an item or person controls us or defines us, it becomes harmful. When you put items before wholeness, your identity relies on those items and they become a hazard to your balance in your mortal experience.

You want richness to compliment your wholeness, not take the place of it. Replacing wholeness with things does not work long term. Wealthy people that first seek wealth without wholeness or a balance within are many times left feeling empty inside. Feel of something missing.

Attachment keeps you from happiness and wholeness. Attachment creates a vulnerable self. Richness simply raises the quality of your earthly experience in all aspects. You can value your material items without attaching to them. Then you can stay in balance and welcome happiness.

Excessiveness becomes detrimental to your being when you define yourself by your possessions, or you attain possessions in order to control others. Do your material things define you? In other words, do your possessions come before your family, connections, humanity, and peace of mind?

A Love-Hate Relationship

Many people unknowingly shy away from or repel money because they consciously or subconsciously believe it is harmful. They seem to have a love-hate relationship with money and sometimes assume wealthy people did something illegal or unethical to get their money.

If someone had the opportunity to live a balanced and whole life, with the choice of abundance or poverty, why would anyone ever willfully choose poverty?

Some people believe too much money will keep them out of heaven. It's my opinion that mindset will only keep one living in lack. Abundance in itself does not violate natural law. How do we determine what is enough or too much money? Where is the balance between money and wholeness?

Having money and material things is not evil. It is the *love* of and attachment to money and things that harm one's spirit. It is how you view and use material wealth that can create toxicity.

Poverty vs. Lack

Some followers believe that poverty is more noble than wealth, so they live in lack. If someone makes a vow to poverty, it must be noble, so they accept that behavior into their belief system. But is poverty noble?

Understand that poverty and lack are not the same. If a religious woman makes a vow of poverty, does this mean she lives in lack? No. Does she break her vow? No. While she may have committed to a vow of poverty, she does not live in lack. She may have lived a poverty lifestyle by choice, but she did not live in lack.

A vow of poverty does not mean that one will go without. It means not focusing a life on material things. No matter how much we have, focusing on wholeness and richness will define how we live our life, having all that we need in the material world.

Lack is going without, such as not having enough food or sufficient healthcare. While those that live in lack live in poverty, those that live at the poverty level are not always living in lack. It is difficult to have wholeness and live in lack. But it is possible to live in poverty and have wholeness.

Lack is a Lesson

Lack is meant to motivate us to aspire us for more in life. It is a lesson. I was raised at the poverty level, and we lacked many things including love, money, security, support, guidance, etc. I learned that was not what I wanted for my life. Lack motivated me.

I don't believe, if given a choice, people would choose lack or poverty over abundance. Seeking wholeness welcomes wisdom. Wisdom welcomes abundance.

It is a terrible waste to believe that poverty or lack is your destiny. All things are possible when you are in harmony with all things.

We Need Richness

Richness offers you options. It gives you more control to create the future you desire. It is your ticket to the future that is your divine right. It allows you the ability to learn and grow to be more well-rounded. With richness, you can more easily create a harmonious environment.

So why do I believe we need richness? Because we are on a physical plain. We only need richness for this temporal experience. It's true, we will not take it with us, but it will give us more opportunities and increase our quality of life while we are here. Contrary to what some believe, one can have abundance without sacrificing wholeness and the spirit self.

Lottery: A Blessing or a Curse?

As we saw in the previous chapter. Winning a lottery is high on the list for attaining happiness. But is it what we expect?

There was a well-respected businessman, we will call him Ted. In 2002 he won over 300-million-dollars on a lottery. In the end, he didn't lose the money, but he lost what he valued most: his peace and harmony, things he possessed before the big win. Not only did the money fail to provide more happiness, but it robbed him of the happiness he had enjoyed before the win.

Believing he was showing love to his granddaughter, he gave her money and cars. The granddaughter turned to drugs and alcohol to deal with the pressure of the new lifestyle. Everyone treated her differently. Soon after, she was found dead. His intent was pure. He loved his granddaughter, but the results were devastating. Often, wealth wakes up the ego in others and attracts envy, betrayal, resentment, jealousy, and many other harmful things into one's life.

We seldom if ever hear about the dark side of a sudden influx of money. Sudden wealth often attracts darkness around us. It can attract chaos, dysfunction, and toxic behaviors from others. Some winners gain money, but many also attract predators. People attempt to swindle them, while others ask to borrow money or invent reasons to sue winners for their money. Some winners end up having to hire bodyguards. The list goes on.

Beware that what seems like a blessing can be a curse and a hardship can be a blessing in disguise. Only through awareness and striving to achieve wholeness will you be able to reliably distinguish a blessing from a curse.

Invest in Yourself.

Each New Skill is Like Buying a Lottery Ticket.

You are Your Own Lottery Win.

Joe Cox, Jr.

End of Life Goal

Our goal in life is not to arrive safely at death but to arrive balanced and whole in all things, with a full life of satisfaction and completeness. If you become properly balanced here on Earth, your life is a job well done. Our goal is to prepare our infinite self for that final day. If you are prepared for your final breath, you will take your happiness with you. The richness of material items will be left behind but the lessons and rich moments we gained with those resources when shared create moments to treasure with family and friends and will forever be embedded within.

First, seek wholeness, then through balance and awareness richness will come to you. Wholeness is your heaven on Earth.

You have no set limit to what you can achieve. The only limits are within you. It's all about what fits your needs and desires. There are always trade-offs. The question is, how do you define richness?

The level of desired abundance is different for everyone. A minimalist can have few material items but see and feel abundance. They may want to spend their life traveling and enjoying nature. Then another might love his work, love living on the ocean, and have his car collection. There is nothing right or wrong with either. It's not about what you accumulate. It's about how and what you do with what you accumulate.

> *Money Does Not Buy Happiness,*
> *but Richness Opens Your World to*
> *Happiness With Abundance*
> *in All Things.*
>
> *Joe Cox, Jr.*

I have every excuse to be living in lack. I chose abundance. This book is not written as a theory. I am your proof of concept.

Losing the Desire for a Great Life

Years ago, in 1956 Earl Nightingale gave a famous speech originally placing it on a vinyl. In his speech "The Strangest Secret," talked of how eager people in their 20's were to make their fortunes. However, by retirement age, only five out of every 100 achieve financial independence. All the others lose their enthusiasm to achieve it. Why? According to Nightingale, it is because we don't think - we conform!

We conform to the 95% that are living life in an unbeneficial way. We don't think. We follow the leader. We do what the majority are doing then wonder why we do not live in a state of happiness.

Conformity is living a fake life. Its living life from the ego. Conformity is living without authenticity. We become whatever we think about. It takes courage to be authentic.

For some reason, the spirit, drive, hope, and desire for abundance at age 20 often fade into survival mode by age 65. The question is, what do the 5% do that the other 95% don't? It is my belief that the 95% do not seek balance. They don't understand the simple concept of attaining wholeness because they don't go looking for it. Instead, they take the easy route, the path of least resistance. The path of losing weight fast or getting rich quickly seldom, if ever, works. When it does, we either regain the weight or lose the money. The fast route is always temporary. The rules to the game of life always prevail.

Wholeness takes work. It's a way of life. Once you attain it, it keeps you thriving in all you do. The key is to never quit when seeking your answers. Be aware. Get your momentum going and keep it going.

Set up your life to follow all natural laws in order to obtain your external desires once your inner wholeness is in balance. This is another secret hidden in plain sight.

Some believe that we can be happy while living in lack. No job, no enthusiasm, no drive, and no goals. But can happiness be found in a lack of motivation and goals? I have never found that to be true. Our spirit does not need physical possessions, but as human beings, we need rich experiences that fill the spirit with great energy.

It's true, our greatest gifts in life are free, but we still need experiences and those often cost money. Our experiences offer valuable lessons. We also have a duty to contribute to humanity through work and services.

When We are Healthy,
We Want a Million Things.
When We are Sick,
We Only Want One Thing.
When We are Unhappy
We Want a Million Things.
When We are Healthy and Happy,
We want Everything But
When We Live in a State of Happiness
We Need Nothing.

Joe Cox, Jr.

To believe you can just quit working and someone will always foot the bill for your food, housing, and travel–is that happiness? Nothing is free in life. When you receive something without equal and fair compensation, a debt is created in the unseen world. There will be a time when natural laws seeks balance and will come for collection.

There are many lessons to be learned through a fulfilling skill or career. We live in a world that requires these external experiences for internal growth.

Financial freedom is not just about having lots of money; it is having a true balance in all material things. That is richness. As long as you have wholeness, then nothing has to be sacrificed to achieve richness.

Now that I am Balanced in All Areas of Life, Happiness and Prosperity are Everywhere I Go.

Joe Cox, Jr.

Summarizing Richness

Who is responsible for your happiness? You! Things will not "make" you happy; they only contribute to your joy through sharing and connection, which is part of richness. Money will not "buy" you happiness, but it does provide more opportunities for growth and experiences that can lead to more richness. The potential is inside you. No one can give you what you don't have within you already.

Gratitude and lack do not coexist. The path to happiness is to wake up with a great attitude, giving gratitude for life and the opportunity you have to live it to the fullest. Be kind to yourself. Invest in yourself to be able to develop a valuable skill set. View all things through the lens of prosperity.

The top regret of elderly people is having lacked the confidence to take risks and live life to the fullest by believing in themselves. Live life with intent and believe in yourself is the lesson. If you live life to the fullest, living in kindness, you will never have regrets in life.

CHAPTER 11

What Creates unHappiness?

We have addressed how to create balance in daily life so we may have wholeness and richness to attract happiness in everything we do. What about common daily situations that can easily knock us off our happiness path?

When we understand the problem, we can fix it. Even if you feel broken, you're not; you're just out of balance. Your goal is to become the best version of yourself. Your personal development is your life's work. Be vigilant and aware of your energy and the energy of others around you in order to rise above difficult situations.

Below are a few things that draw us away from balance and what we can do about it. You can protect yourself when you know what to look for.

Where Does Change Come From?

As the saying goes, "Want to change the world? Begin with yourself." If everyone changed themselves for the better, raising humanity's collective consciousness, the world's problems would be solved. Too many people are worried about controlling others more than themselves. Attempting to force or control the outside world is not what causes change. Frustration and chaos are the only result when attempting to change anyone outside of the self. Happiness will always elude you if your happiness is dependent on someone or something outside of you.

Your View of Life

Positivity is one of the best and easiest methods by far to keep away the unhappiness bugs throughout the day. Look at each day as an opportunity for a new lesson to gain wisdom. You can't think yourself into happiness, but you can decide to have a happy and positive attitude. Your attitude reflects your belief system.

Start your day with an attitude of gratitude. Program positivity into your belief system. Begin every day by giving thanks for what you now have, no matter how little you have. Remember that life happens *for* you, not against you. A positive attitude will help manifest what you want in your future. Make positivity a way of life. It will open unlimited opportunities for you. It is the beginning of attracting happiness in all you do.

Order and Structure

Order and structure welcome happiness. One must be organized in their life to be balanced. Choose a system of organization and follow it daily. Begin placing your life in order with the simple steps of making your bed and organizing your space each morning. Structure your day with a plan of action. These actions are the foundation to balance.

Self-motivation and self-control makes the person. One without discipline is a child full of reactions, rather than a mature and balanced adult in control of their life.

Joe Cox, Jr.

Self-Comparison

Comparing yourself to another is like comparing an orange and an apple. It's pointless because one is unique to the other. That is why it is self-sabotaging. Nothing positive or productive comes from comparing yourself to others. You were born the perfect you.

Do you think the orange would say to the apple, "I wish I was red?" The apple is a perfect apple. The orange is a perfect orange. You are the perfect you; now become the *best* you. Yes, we all desire to better ourselves. Becoming better is a natural instinct that is built into your essence because seeking growth is necessary for your happiness. Comparing is not improving; it is self-judgment.

Comparing ourselves to others creates a problem that only exists in our minds. In this circumstance, the ego is working against your development and growth. This creates an imbalance of the mind, which leads you away from wholeness.

Comparing yourself to others is a guaranteed way to create unhappiness. Not accepting yourself is the fast lane to misery. Instead, make your daily mantra, "I am enough."

Love yourself today for who you are and focus on being the best you. Nobody can be a better you than you.

Be Authentic

What is an authentic person? Authentic people love themselves. They have a belief system with a solid structure and a life of virtues and integrity. Authentic people value their potential and are willing to work to develop themselves. They are in control of themselves and feel no need to control or seek validation from others.

Being authentic means connecting to your higher self. Being authentic is following your intuition and always listening to your gut. Being authentic means going after the career path you want, not the one that others tell you to pursue. It means gaining the education to work in an industry that fits your personality and your goals.

Authentic people set high standards when it comes to friendship. They only accept friends who best complement their personality, virtues, and values. Being authentic is not curbing or lowering your standard just to have more friends.

Authentic people may have fewer friends but they enjoy deeper connections.

The ego will pull you away from your authenticity if you allow it. It is the voice of self-judgment. The ego is self-destructive. The ego knows that in order to get control, it must first beat you down. Control your ego and you will control your life.

Not being yourself is miserable. How can anyone be authentic while failing to see their own value? We cannot be our authentic selves if we want to be someone else or if we are trying to please everyone by being what they want us to be. Avoid people-pleasing.

You may not like or accept the situation you were born into, but you have control of everything within you including your personality, your integrity, your attitude, and your character and drive to become the best you.

It is constructive to recognize the virtues or qualities in others that you would like to develop. Adopt those qualities while maintaining your authenticity. Be authentic in all you do. Authenticity attracts happiness.

Embrace yourself and don't worry what others think about you. Self-acceptance is imperative to becoming your authentic self. Those that worry about what others think place themselves in mental bondage. They become a prisoner of others' opinions. To become your authentic self you must completely accept and be comfortable with yourself as you are.

You know you're living in authenticity when you lay your head on your pillow at night and you are comfortable with who you are. You enjoy the progress you're making in life. You love yourself. Balance in all things will get you there. If you are not in balance within yourself, this is a good time to think, *How can I do a better job tomorrow?*

Looking Outside Yourself

Many people look only outside themselves for their happiness, but they are looking where happiness can't be found. It all begins within you.

Many people seek happiness in material items. Most don't realize they are trying to fill the empty void inside their spirits with money, new cars, dating, or looking cool. Your happiness originates from within through wholeness. Wholeness allows you to fill that emptiness within. Wholeness gives material items meaning. It's not the jet ski that gives life meaning; it is sharing and enjoying the jet ski that creates connections that give the experience its meaning.

Wants versus Needs

Most people have no idea what they want. Many think they know what they want but get it and still are not happy and not sure why. Some try to fill their emptiness with material items. That discontented urge is the ego saying "Gimmie, gimmie." Your ego determines what you want in the now. There is no depth to the ego. No gameplan. Everything the ego wants is junk to the spirit self.

The ego craves "junk emotions." Pleasure in the place of love is "junk pleasure". It's living only from the body, only engaging in shallow feelings in an attempt to fill the inside void. The ego seeks "feel good" emotions that never last. We operate through the ego when we lack awareness.

Your ego seeks wants. Your intuition knows what you need. Have pure intent and your intuition will show you everything you need for the quality of life you desire. It will attract what you need through your awareness.

Worry

Why do we worry? People worry only when they feel they have little or no control over a situation. Worry comes when we fear the worst and believe that life is not working for us. We manifest the very thing we fear by worrying about it. Worry is manifesting negative things into our lives.

Nothing good comes from worrying. Worry is deconstructive and unbeneficial. It produces nothing positive. You either have control of a situation or you don't. If it's something occurring within you, then you don't need to worry because you have control of everything within you. If it's something outside of you, there's no need to worry because you have no control over anything outside you and everything is working for your benefit anyway.

A common worry for parents is a concern for their grown children. It's not a parent's place to worry about their grown children. Allow them to take a hit for their personal growth. Teach them true principles while they are young and then love them by allowing them to make mistakes. Raising a stable child is not protecting them from the obstacle, it is teaching and allowing them to overcome obstacles on their own.

When you worry about others, you keep yourself away from your own wholeness and happiness and you interfere with the path of the person you're worried about. Worry is a negative force on your wholeness.

The day you realize that everything happens at the perfect time, in the perfect place, for the proper reason, is the day you set yourself free from worry.

Dwelling on the Past

Dwelling on a negative past causes you to live your today as if you were still in that past situation of yesterday. Same dysfunction, different day, with the same dysfunctional result. Living today in the past leads to continual misery. Continuous thoughts of the past only result in your future reflecting that past. We remember the past for only one purpose: to help us grow by learning from its life lessons.

Live for today, learning lessons from yesterday, while planning for the future.

Joe Cox

Only look at the past to learn the lessons. Nothing more. Making peace with your past is done through self-forgiveness and acceptance. This is the process of letting go and releasing. This opens the doors to all good things.

Thought Loops of the Past

Many people get caught in the "thought loops" of yesterday. Thought loops are like mental movies replayed over and over again. They trap you within your own life. They keep many of us down. Why would you watch the same movie over and over knowing you're going to be sad and cry every time? If you don't like that movie of the past, change the channel! You can change the channel by looking at your life differently.

Become Thankful for Your Past

What if we begin to be thankful for our troubled pasts? Follow me here for a moment. What if you woke up one morning and you could not remember anything negative from your past? Only the good stuff. Sounds great, right? But without those past negative moments or lessons, how would you know how to make better decisions today? You would have nothing to compare your current options with, nothing to learn from. Chances are you would probably begin making the same mistakes, recreating your negative past all over again. There is a reason you made those mistakes. We all need our past mistakes to gain perspective and develop wisdom.

Be grateful for your past. We all need our past mistakes to inform our future choices. Be grateful that those mistakes are in your past, so they need not be in your future. Learn from your past so you can live today in abundance.

"Failure"

Let's talk about the word failure. The common perspective in the United States regarding failure is typically formed from our approach to testing and grading in our education systems. In school, the pass/fail approach may work fine. It is a way of checking students' progress. The issue is that a pass/fail approach conditions us to believe the word failure applies to real life. Nobody tells us after graduation to forget the pass/fail system. The real world does not operate that way.

I think this is one reason that many teenagers struggle after high school. They become conditioned to grading everything they do. Self-judgment is one of the results, and they begin to wonder if they pass or fail as a person. Some kids see themselves as failures no matter what they accomplish. They don't realize that life outside of the classroom is a different system of approach. Approach real life with a pass or fail system and you will be miserable.

Not succeeding and failing are not the same thing. Failure is a self-sabotaging concept, a toxic lens through which we often judge our progress and achievements. It implies a defined final result. In real life, you only fail if you quit. Think of life as an open-book test. There is always an answer, you just have to do the work to find it.

In life, trying and not getting it right is not failing; it is a mistake, an oops, a blunder, or trial and error - whatever you want to call it. It is what happens as you walk your path. It is learning through experience what does not work. There is a difference. Failure implies that you have reached the end, the final result. Nothing is final in your earth experience until your spirit leaves your body. Without fearing failure, you can trust that you have every reason to try. The mistake is where the greatest wisdom is found. That is why I removed the word failure from my vocabulary.

"Success"

Now let's look at the word success. The typical concept of success is the extreme on the other end of the spectrum from failure, which is also self-sabotaging. It gives us a false sense of having reached our final destination, a destination of personal influence. In this understanding of success, you earn respect, become lovable, and begin to feel like you are enough. The problem is, this "success" is conditioned on your level of wealth, particularly the amount of money in your bank account.

I fell for the success myth only to be disappointed and left picking up the pieces of my life. I was working and waiting for happiness, not realizing that I was already rich because of how I approached life. I was lacking wholeness and didn't know it. I could not see the reality of my situation because I was out of balance. I lacked the awareness to know. When happiness did not come, I thought I had done something wrong. I thought I had failed. In reality, I had just made a mistake because I was missing information and didn't know if there were answers. At the time I had not yet learned about wholeness. I was not fulfilled because I was not whole within.

Life is not about being a "success." Success is a behavior, not a destination. The problem is we look at happiness as a condition of success. Success is not a requirement for happiness, but achievements are conditions of richness that welcome happiness.

How do you know if a person is successful? Who defines it? It's not related to money, though our modern society wants you to believe it is. Remember, richness and wealth are not the same thing.

The ego loves the way the world defines success with flash and money. The dictionary defines success as "the accomplishment of an aim or purpose." Success is not a destination; it is a state of being. A group of people that help the homeless population off the streets may be successful in their efforts, but not considered successful by some because the content of their bank accounts is only average.

As I moved forward on my path, I began replacing the word success with the word achievements or accomplishments. Achievement means that you have reached a new level. It's a growth mindset, always saying, *"Now that I've gotten this far, I'll begin working on the next level and achieve the next stage in life.*

You are successful when you're working toward your next achievement, looking for answers, working on your goals, and accepting yourself today as whole, always working to be stronger in mind, body, and spirit.

If you get to the destination of modern success and say, *Now what?* then you have lost your way. From this point, you either allow the ego to rule you through ostentatious behavior or get stuck trying to figure out where to go from there. This is a sign that you overlooked wholeness along the way.

Successful behavior focuses on progress, such as building up your resilience, attracting happiness, and progressing toward your goals. Setting and achieving goals keeps us focused on self-improvement and personal growth. Achieve one goal, then begin another. This focus keeps your compass pointing in the right direction. Once you enjoy prosperity, find a need in the world and fill it with your support. Give back to your community and help guide others to their path in life. Create a product or service from the lessons you learn in life. People will pay for things that raise them up in life. Create an environment for others to do that.

You can have money and not be successful. You can be successful and not have money. A mother that raises her children to love themselves and contribute to the world is a tremendous success, but mothers get very little recognition because of how the world defines success.

The world deceives us when it insists that money and success are the same. Success is the attitude with which you approach life, always focused on your end game. Success is your graduation from this life, the day you take your last breath, knowing you took care of your family, you treated people with kindness, you stayed in harmony with life, and you made a difference by being an example to others. Your infinite self grew and benefited from your world experience - that is a successful life.

In summary, this is why neither "failure" nor "success" is in my vocabulary. These two words refer to the extremes on opposite ends of a spectrum. I finally realized operating at extremes opposes balance.

Quitting

I was told that if I start something I should always finish it or I am a quitter. That philosophy is confusing. The definition of a quitter states, "a person who gives up easily or does not have the courage or determination to finish a task." However, what if you realize that what you are striving for is not beneficial to you? That definition puts you into a catch-22. It appears you are either stuck doing something you don't find beneficial or you're a quitter.

Imagine that you start playing a new sport or learning a new skill. You discover that you don't enjoy the new venture that you've been practicing, so you abandon the effort. Your decision to stop something that you don't find beneficial to you doesn't mean you have become a quitter. It only means you want to do something different with your time, which is a completely valid desire. Choosing a different direction is called a "stop loss." If you understand that you can quit something without any shame because you don't find it to be beneficial, you're more likely to try more new ventures. Openness to new experiences is how you learn and develop. If you try something but realize that your time would be better spent doing something different, then that is awareness, not quitting.

Never quitting means to keep moving forward in life, whatever moving forward looks like for you. Only you can decide the most beneficial way to move forward in your life.

When you recognize that you never fail or quit at anything if you are still trying to better yourself then your life will blossom and become beautiful.

Making Excuses

I have heard every excuse. Is there such a thing as a good excuse? I was once the leader of a real estate team that was consistently underperforming. After working with them, I could not understand why their performance was so lacking. I gave them every opportunity for growth. They had excuses for everything. I was spending more time trying to help them than doing my own work. After a while, I realized I was trying to help them more than they were willing to help themselves. I finally fired them all, then, Boom! My productivity exploded. Their excuses were hindering my abilities and achievements.

Leaders never make excuses; they find answers. Unaccountable and irresponsible people make excuses.

After running a thrift store to benefit the local homeless population for a while, I learned a lot about the homeless. One thing I consistently noticed was that they had been conditioned to believe their situation was unavoidable. I have heard every excuse in the book for living on the street, the most common being a need for someone else to validate one's worthiness. No one loved them.

They failed to understand that one must have self-love first, which was a hard lesson for me to learn too. They based their worth and potential on how others viewed them. With that self-limiting perspective, they were unable to accept themselves and create a productive life.

With my background, I could have used excuses to be homeless, an addict, or to otherwise give up. Instead, I chose to rise above it. I was always looking for answers. I accepted personal accountability. Today I have been rewarded with amazing opportunities and happiness in my life because I sought those answers.

I choose to rise above it.

Joe Cox, Jr.

Excuses block development. The proper way to process an excuse is when you think of an excuse, then immediately try to think of the resolution to that excuse. I tell my employees not to come to me with an excuse, instead come to me with an issue and the best way to resolve it.

When you make mistakes, don't make excuses. Accept it. Own it. Look for the lesson. Mistakes are part of life. If you're continually working to better yourself, then life is much more enjoyable. Taking control of your life brings amazing results.

Complaining

Have you ever been around someone who complains about everything? If you complain or are around someone who complains you are welcoming toxicity.

If you are around a complainer, just walk away. Complaining is not constructive or instructive. Low-energy people love to dwell in toxic energy. If one takes proper action by addressing a problem and fixing it, there is nothing to complain about. Complaining is simply swimming in one's own self-pity and victimhood, crying out to others for sympathy or an excuse to not better oneself.

Complaining does not find a solution. It only welcomes misery and unhappiness to all participants. If you are always looking for a solution then there is nothing to complain about.

Boundaries

What are personal boundaries and when do we need them? Personal boundaries are limitations on how we allow others into our lives. We need boundaries when others attempt to inflict upon us any type of action that is out of harmony with who we are for the sake of self-care. No one ever has the right to disrespect you, harm you, or bring you down by forcing chaos into your life, not even your family.

Become a giving person but maintain healthy boundaries. Love your family but maintain distance and boundaries from any toxic relatives.

Loving unconditionally does not require you to discard boundaries and make yourself vulnerable to toxic behavior. Never trust anyone blindly. Follow your intuition. Protect yourself.

Help But Don't Carry

Part of your wholeness is to help others, but to help others more than they are willing to help themselves is detrimental to your welfare and it violates allowing others to walk their own path. Don't try to rescue another. I cannot rescue you. You can only rescue yourself. I can only guide you to water; it is up to you to drink.

Giving Away Your Power

Whenever you accept a toxic situation into your life, you give away your power. When you give away your power you give away your peace and harmony. The most common way to give away your power is to be offended. When you are offended, you accept the information that you are told as if it were true. You are taking it personally. Most issues with others are not about you but about them. Don't take anything personally. That is only accepting detrimental energy into your life. You don't ever have to defend a lie, and the truth will defend itself.

Self-Projection

Each person shows how they feel about themselves through their own behavior. Pay attention when communicating with someone. Foolish people will say negative things. Wise people will say positive things.

We tell the world who we are by the way we treat others. Say someone tells you that you're stupid. If there is no truth to that, there is no need to defend yourself. Just smile and walk away because they are just telling you how they feel about themselves. Their behavior says everything about them. Likewise, be aware of what you say to others. Your behavior tells the world how you view yourself.

Eliminate Disappointment

Did you know that you have the power to never be disappointed? Expectations are great deliverers of misery. Set up your whole life to eliminate disappointment by not expecting specific behaviors from others. Expectations are an attempt to control an outcome. Let things go. Let people be themselves. Let things flow as they may and keep yourself whole.

Understanding Triggers

Most people from toxic backgrounds have triggers. A trigger is something or someone that causes an emotional reaction within yourself by refreshing the moment of past trauma. It takes you back to a moment of those feelings and emotions. It can be a smell, a sound, or anything else that engages your senses and connects to a negative, painful memory.

> *The deeper the pain, the greater impact,*
> *the greater the lesson.*
>
> Joe Cox, Jr.

A trigger is a learning opportunity. There are many lessons in triggers. To help get control of them, look for the lesson. We will explore how to release those negative emotions to rid you of triggers in the next chapter.

Summary of unHappiness

The goal is to align yourself with the natural laws that regulate life. Make that alignment your way of life. It begins with your wholeness in all things.

So, if you have never questioned your belief system, this is a good time to do that. Your belief system regulates every choice and thought in your life. If you have no idea why you believe what you do, how is it *your* belief system?

Become more aware of what you do and why you do it. No one is perfect, but we can all do better. Life is not a sprint. We are in it for the long run. We are all our own self-projects. Review your life and work through one issue at a time - one step at a time.

Remember, if you understand something you can handle it. It is not up to you to change others. Too many people believe that controlling others is where they will find happiness. They believe they are "fixing" other people, when, in fact, they are just holding up a mirror to themselves. That approach never works. We must do what we can to better ourselves and hope our energy influences others for good, but ultimately, change rests in the hands of each individual.

> ***It's not where you are in life that matters,***
> ***but how far you have had to come to***
> ***get where you are.***
>
> *Joe Cox, Jr.*

CHAPTER 12

Life-Changing Experience

Have you ever been in so much emotional pain that you couldn't think straight and didn't know what to do about it? It can be very debilitating. Often, emotional pain seems to hurt more and last longer than any physical pain. You can take a pill or get a shot for physical pain, but mental and emotional anguish is not so easily managed. However, we humans can handle anything once we understand it.

I learned to keep an open mind regarding various healing methods, even those outside of what our society calls "normal". This choice was life-changing for me. Valid answers changed everything for me.

I was working 12 hours a day, six days a week as a real estate agent, and loved my job. It is true that if you love your job, you will never work a day in your life. I believe loving what

I do contributed to me beating the odds of my childhood. At 35 years old, I was a millionaire and owned a portfolio of rental properties.

My path was very different from the people I grew up around. I didn't work for money. I learned how to make money work for me. I was purchasing investment properties and doing very well in my business. I learned all about money. Money seemed to flow to me. I had "the golden touch", but something was still missing.

At the end of the day, when everything was silent, an emptiness would visit me, a void and a pain so deep it was agonizing. I carried it with me for so long it was my normal. I just thought I was flawed and that was just the way it was.

At the time, my social awareness was very low. I had a difficult time developing quality relationships. I was great with clients but on a personal level, I still had issues. In fact, I only attracted toxic relationships outside of work.

My professional relationships were different. The internet was in its infancy so observing others in real life was the only means I had available to learn what a functional family was supposed to be.

I met wealthy people. I hung around them and became the average of those I hung around. They were completely different from anyone I had known from childhood. I realized that my wealthy connections had families they loved and supported, people in their lives who loved them, but I didn't. I also noticed some miserable millionaires. They were usually making money, not for the sake of providing for their families or with any interest in contributing to society, but for the sake of wealth itself. They were often grouchy, critical, arrogant, and didn't walk with confidence, always boasting of their own success and intelligence. Many of them also saw deceitful business practices as acceptable. I can see now that was their ego talking.

I lacked positive connections. I didn't have any close bonds from childhood and lacked the love that a functional family would have offered. Being single, I was fine with being alone, but the loneliness was eating at me. Being alone is physical. Being lonely is that unmet need for connection, the same loneliness I felt as a child. I needed to share my life with someone. People were all around me, but I really had no one. I could only assume then, as I had when I was young, that something was wrong with me. Maybe it was just confirming that I was too flawed for relationships. As I solved the problem of money, all my other problems just seemed so much larger.

I had been away from my birth family for years while I built my real estate career. I thought maybe it was time I shared my knowledge with them. I wanted to help them have a better life.

Helping Family

I went back to my family, the family I was given, and offered to teach them what I had learned, believing they would appreciate my efforts. I thought that fixing my family would show my gratitude for what I had received. So, I went to work. I planned and paid for a fishing trip to Destin, Florida. My whole birth family was invited. My goal was to build a bond with them, the bond we had never shared in the past.

Most joined in the trip. I began offering them investment opportunities. I helped them purchase various properties. It didn't take long for the problems to begin. It started because I was helping them more than they were willing to help themselves.

Everyone in my family thought differently. I was expecting more out of them than they expected from themselves. I now realize that is why they are the way they are in the first place. They sat back and waited for the money to come in. I was trying to force my drive and motivation onto them and it was not working. They had no problem allowing me to do the work. About the time I realized the truth of the situation.

What Happened to Me?

Trust was broken when a deed was manipulated by my own family, cutting me out of the real estate I owned. I could not comprehend it. I confronted my father. It was not the crime or the amount that hurt me, it was my own father laughing as he walked away with a smirk I will never forget. He had betrayed me as a child. I had forgiven him and let him back into my life. I believed he had changed. I gave trust without it being earned.

Then, BAM! As soon as I realized the betrayal, that I had been played for a fool, my body and mind began shutting down. I could barely function. My motivation was gone. My spirit was broken. I could barely get out of bed. I had no appetite, and when I did eat, the food had no taste. Shock engulfed me.

Looking back, it is clear that my balance was thrown out of whack. This was when darkness came to visit and would not leave. My "dark night of the soul" had begun. At the time I didn't know what was happening.

For 10 years, I was a workaholic and lost myself in my work. Success was my motivation and a distraction from my issues because I thought it would bring me the happiness and fulfillment I needed. Everyone would love me if I were successful, right? When that didn't happen, I lost what I thought was myself. My mind felt like it had been put in a mixer.

I went from being a high-producing real estate agent working 12 hours a day to not caring what day it was almost overnight. I was in an abyss, a void that lingered. I had no desire to get out of my recliner. I would stare at the TV without turning it on. I felt numb. My meaning, my purpose, and my energy all dissolved overnight. But what happened to *me*?

The Shutdown

The shock was more than a mind could handle. It was like my mind and my spirit were no longer working together. Consciously I knew what had happened, but I could not think my way out of the situation. I had always followed the saying "The strong shall survive." I was determined to never be weak and never give up, but something was happening inside me beyond my conscious control. For the first time as an adult, I was lost, and I had no one to turn to for help.

My business phone would ring, and I would cringe as it threatened my isolation. I had no choice but to put my real estate career on hold until I could get a grip on myself. I thought,

Surely I can work through this over the next few weeks. The days went by in a fog. My depression seemed to be getting worse. Isolation was both my friend and my enemy. The days turned into weeks, weeks turned into months and months turned into years. I attempted new ventures, but they all collapsed. My heart did not seem to be interested in anything anymore. My life force was deteriorating. My will to live was hanging on by a thread. In the past, everything I touched had seemed to turn into gold but now it seems everything I touched turned into crap. I was making one poor decision after another, slowly losing my grip on life.

I had been working to become successful thinking that my self-worth or worthiness of being loved would automatically increase with financial wealth. I made my worthiness of love conditional on my success, not understanding how love functions. I believed that one day I would be worthy of love and that happiness would suddenly show up to the party in my head. I was looking outside of me for answers, but the pain was deep within me somewhere.

The Denial

Rather than healing, in the past I had used denial to move forward in life, which now reinvited the depression. Denial would no longer work. This time I was forced to face my fears. All the emotions and pain of my traumatic childhood came flooding back. In my mind, no matter how much money or success I earned, I was still that same wounded and flawed child. No matter where I went, I followed. I could not run from myself, so my problems followed too.

After I had accomplished so much, I still lived in lack. I lacked the balance of something within me but I had no idea how to gain it. I didn't even know what I was trying to balance. I thought that if I ignored my pain, or just "let it go" and forgot about it, it would go away. That didn't work. With no answers in sight, for the first time in my life, I turned to the bottle to help numb the pain within myself. I had taken pride in having stayed clean of drugs and alcohol. This time the pain inside was too great.

Depression had been my comfort zone as a child. It was the only thing I had known. I had abandoned my depression but never dealt with it. It was like the depression was laughing at me, mocking me, punishing me for leaving.

My life was tumbling, and I had no idea how to stop it this time. Was my life worth fighting for? After 35 years, I was so tired of the struggle. I was so tired of not having the answers.

To the outside world, I was successful. I was in the top 1% of successful people in the United States financially, but on the inside, I felt worthless and broken, like I was drowning. I began to think, *Maybe there are no answers. Maybe this is all just a trick to torture us humans.*

I could no longer work. I lost interest in my daily routine and productive habits. My spirit tumbled for years until I lost all my material possessions and had to file for bankruptcy. I struggled with the idea of taking my own life numerous times. In my mind, I wanted to live but it appeared life was set up so I could not win. I thought I was too broken and flawed to win. Happiness did not exist in my world. It was not that I wanted to die; I just wanted the pain to stop. Over the years, I felt that

I had tried everything. But I still had a void within that I could not fill.

I tried therapists, one after the other. I tried different medications. They may have numbed me, but still nothing improved. I was so distraught. This phase of my life seemed to have no end in sight.

After trying traditional healing approaches without success, I was at my wit's end with only one thought, that I was broken and I could not be fixed. I began to make plans to end my life. I began giving away every material item I had left. I began to plan the details.

Plans to an Ending

I sat alone. After 12 years of being mentally trapped in a hell I could not escape, I was giving up for good - the letters were written, the plan was set. Nobody would miss me. I thought I was doing the world a favor. Just at that moment, my phone rang. It distracted me.

I had not received a phone call in weeks. I answered with tears in my eyes, it was my cousin, Steve. He was happy and upbeat about life, an energy I had not felt in many years. I started to talk in a broken voice with tears now streaming down my cheek. He asked if I wanted to talk later. I said, "No, please stay on the phone and keep talking." We talked for an hour. I mostly listened. Looking back, a connection was all I needed at that time to hold on a little longer. After the call, without thinking about it, I put everything away like it was routine. Something in me had been satisfied. I no longer thought of taking my life at that moment. A glimmer of hope and a little good energy was enough to stop me from giving up that day.

For the first time in years, my cousin inspired me to reach out for help. I had been trying to fix everything on my own like most guys do. When I asked for help, things slowly began to change.

After many years of living in emotional darkness, I was exhausted from the struggle. I was desperate. I read everything I could, trying to sort myself out. I felt like a big ball of toxic emotions. All I could do was just exist. After leaving home at age 16, I found that spark for life but then lost it again. I thought, *Did I miss something?* I wanted to live life to the fullest, but depression was draining the life energy out of me.

I knew I had to do something different. Negative thoughts dominated my being. I was desperate for answers. The same question continued. What had happened to me?

I had done what the self-help books had said to do: forgive, let it go... I no longer felt anger toward my family, but I was still struggling. I learned that while we may consciously let go of pain, sometimes our subconscious minds need help to remove the toxic energy behind our pain.

The first turning point that gave me hope was a therapist that listened to me on a deeper level. At the end of the session, rather than giving me a pill, she hugged me and told me everything was going to be OK. She was the only person who had ever hugged me and told me that, *ever*! That simple act of kindness changed something within me. It touched my spirit.

Then soon after I heard about something called trapped emotions. It sounded a little strange, but I investigated. Here is what I learned about trapped emotions:

Trapped in Me

A trapped emotion is an energy that becomes trapped within us during a traumatic event such as neglect, abuse, betrayal, etc. This happens when we are ill equipped to process toxic emotions properly. Without processing an emotion properly, we can hold on to the emotional pain caused by a trauma and that pain can stay trapped within our bodies. It manifests itself through the physical body with symptoms such as low energy, anxiety, depression, and disease.

Trauma energy in the body has been documented through the work of various medical doctors including Dr. Gabor Mate in the book "The Myth of Normal" and Dr. Bessel Van Der Kolk in the book "The Body Keeps the Score."

There are practitioners in different modalities that can treat and release trapped emotions. I read about this process, and I thought, *Could it be that I have trapped emotions from my childhood trauma?* That had to be it. I found a book that explained these concepts in a simple format called "The Emotion Code", by Dr. Bradley Nelson. That book gave me hope for the first time in years.

After reading the book, I took action. I reached out for help. The session lasted about an hour. After the first session, the practitioner reminded me that I would experience a processing period. This period typically lasts up to five days after a session and allows the body to rebalance the spirit energy after trapped emotions are released. They could only release a certain number of emotions at each session. As with any healing, it takes time. I was not sure what happened, but I felt a shift of some kind deep within me. I felt just a little lighter. About 24 hours later I became nauseated. Fortunately, that common reaction only lasts about an hour and provides a lot of relief.

I had another session about a week later. I felt a little lighter again, and like clockwork, the nausea happened again. I thought to myself, *There is no way that's coincidental.* Something was really happening. I was healing from the inside out without medication. After years of feeling lost and broken, these changes gave me hope.

The Comeback Story

While still in emotion code therapy, I was running a thrift store for the homeless. I had once read, "If you want to find yourself, lose yourself in the service of others." I sold the only thing I had left and cashed in my life insurance policy. I had spent everything I had trying to find me and fix me.

I was running the store and living in a small town in northern Georgia, 70 miles from where I grew up. About 10 weeks after I opened the thrift store, I was online one night connecting with some folks, organizing donations for the store when I noticed a face I had not seen in over 30 years. I couldn't believe it. Remember that beautiful little girl that I danced with when I was 15 years old? That angel! It was her! The one I was told I was not worthy of. I noticed she was single and living in my town!

I reached out to her with a simple message to see if she'd like to meet for lunch and catch up as old friends. She agreed; I had no idea what to expect. We decided to meet at a little outdoor café. I had not yet heard her voice; all arrangements were made through messaging and texting.

As I walked from the parking lot into the little café, it was like everything slowed down. The parking lot seemed a mile long. I could see the smile on her beautiful face as I finally reached her. She held her arms out for a hug and I grabbed her and held her tight. The people at the café no longer existed. Everything was happening in slow motion... she looked up at me, and I said to her "There you are." It was like coming home. I knew with every fiber of my being she was what had been missing in my life all this time. I had never had love and love from her radiated. That angel was in my arms and I was not letting go this time.

On that beautiful sunny day, we talked for hours. My internal guidance system showed me the answers I had been seeking. I was home, home with my angel on earth, my purpose, my meaning, my everything. As we talked, I realized she had already been through her dark night of the soul, and she could understand me as no one else could. Tears poured from both of us. I knew deep within this was the girl I was supposed to be married to all along. My other half. My soulmate.

Life felt lighter as our relationship began defining itself. We talked as often as we could then I asked her to help at the store. We worked together for about a year, healing ourselves and running the store, knowing we would never leave one another. Then it came time to prepare for our life together.

That day finally arrived - we got married! It's the best thing I have ever done for myself. At 15 years old, my heart told me she was my soul mate, my twin flame, but outside voices told me I was unworthy. Later, she explained that she had felt the same way about me all those years ago. Lesson: Never allow ANYONE else to define you, no matter your age.

After our marriage, we closed the store and began to build a new life together, starting from scratch. I worked hard and after a couple years of healing inside and out, I finally got back to the work I loved in real estate. My goal was to be the highest-selling sales associate in my office. After 15 years, my spark was back, and my "golden touch" was back.

During my first full calendar year back in real estate, I worked to become the top performer in my brokerage office, winning awards, and producing one million dollars in gross commission income. That is 10 times the average agent.

What I learned

It is amazing what we can do without the weight of the world on us! *You* can rise above it, heal, and thrive in all you do. The secret is that happiness comes from finding that balance in all things. You have a divine right to balance and happiness. Your happiness benefits you and everyone around you.

I always said to my myself, *I can handle anything life deals me as long as it's not in vain.* That is what kept me looking for the lesson.

You have every opportunity available to you! I hope my story will inspire you to always keep your heart and mind open and ask for the guidance you need throughout your life.

Someone once told me that to find happiness, *you already have everything you need within you.* At the time, I thought they were crazy. They would not have said that to me if they had known how broken I was inside.

Now I know they were right and I was never broken. I was simply out of balance. Everything I ever needed was within me. I just needed the love, support and connection to help me bring it out.

You have everything you need within you. I hope sharing my story will help you to connect with your own greatness.

You Are Not Broken,
You Are Just Out of Balance.

Joe Cox, Jr.

CHAPTER 13

Why suicide is not an option!

Suicide has always been a taboo subject. Could that be because we imagine that if we don't talk about it, then it won't happen? If things worked like that, most of our problems would disappear, but we know that is not how problems get resolved. Confronting issues resolves issues.

I know this can be a difficult subject to talk about. The good news is suicide is preventable. Over the last couple of decades, we have made much progress in awareness. However, it is evident the message is not always getting through. Annual suicide rates continue to rise. Obviously, some people continue to view suicide as a valid option.

For most people, even the thought of someone taking their own life is difficult to comprehend. It is heartbreaking. It is imperative that we come to understand more about this subject and why too many people see this option as their only way to get the relief they seek.

For me, growing up in chaos, life never felt safe. I went years not knowing if there were valid answers or strategies to solving life's problems. I believed that I was somehow broken. After many years of searching, I began finding answers. I now understand. I could finally take action to heal. Through healing, I feel safe and connected, and I thrive with abundance in all things. My past had a purpose. I now give gratitude for my past because I understand it. The lessons from my past now give me the ability to help others, including you.

Awareness

Suicide awareness today is everywhere, so why is it not solving the problem? We continue to do the same things with suicide prevention and treatment and keep getting the same results. Maybe it's time to try something new, to add a new, proven approach for healing to how we currently promote awareness and healing.

We must begin teaching a more proactive approach to suicide prevention. We need to instill within the belief system of each individual that suicide is not an option. It's not on the menu. The goal is to create a general awareness that removes suicide as an option before an individual's dark thoughts ever occur. That is much easier to accomplish if we know there are valid solutions to whatever problems we face.

Being able to validate their feelings and offer real assurance that their pain can be healed in this life, through proven healing methods, changes everything. Traditional therapy is often wonderful for helping provide immediate relief but is not usually as successful regarding long-term healing.

Most parents, teachers, relatives, and friends want to help a loved one who appears potentially suicidal, but unless you have been there, it's difficult to understand what is going on in that person's head and spirit. We are talking about intense mental, emotional, and spiritual pain so deep that most people can't recognize or understand it. I have been there. I assure you that the pain is real and it is deep.

> ### *Suicide is not an option.*
>
> *Joe Cox, Jr.*

The way we have been treating mental health in Western society is similar to how we maintain our cars. The engine represents our body. Oil represents our spirit-mind connection. The fuel represents our energy.

If our psychological oil is low, we fill up with a talk therapy session. A week later, it is low again, so we fill up again with another session. The oil leak is not getting better. We are giving our cars care and treatment but not fixing the root cause so we are not necessarily getting better. The real question is, what is causing the oil to leak out of the car? What is causing your unseen pain? You will never find the problem just looking at the mind and body.

Suicide is Not Just a Body and Mind Issue

Mental confusion contributes to a broken spirit and an emotionally disconnected heart. Confusion disrupts the harmony between the mind, body, and spirit. A broken spirit creates a low consciousness level. Your consciousness is where you connect to the essence of your authentic self. A low consciousness in turn creates toxic behavior out of harmony with your will to live, or your life force, thereby creating an imbalance of wholeness. Continual energy imbalances maintain an alignment out of harmony with self, preventing one from healing. We need a suicide prevention method that initiates healing. What catalyst initiates healing? Clarity of why and where the problem originated! Why is your oil leaking? What is the root cause?

Clarity comes by recognizing and understanding the root problem and gaining the knowledge for authentic steps to healing. A lack of knowledge in this area was the main reason my dark night of the soul lasted so long. Once I discovered where to start, I could feel my healing begin from day one. I found a simple non-evasive process because my desire to heal was so great.

What burdened me were the trapped emotions I mentioned previously. Toxic emotions trapped within us keep us out of balance in mind, body, and spirit, making wholeness unattainable. Your spiritual self wants to heal and has a natural desire for homeostasis. When you have trapped emotions, your entire being cannot function optimally.

Wholeness is key to healing. Sickness manifests in the mind and body through anxiety, depression, and many other forms of illness. The connection to self is ignored. Trapped emotions are your obstacles to healing. Remove the trapped emotions, then balance will come naturally. Your body will attain homeostasis in mind body and spirit. With homeostasis, we have no desire for self-harm.

We know the body is capable of natural healing, but what if you step on a nail? Will it heal if you don't remove the nail? No, not only will it not heal, but it will fester and get worse. It's the same with trapped emotions. Your mind and spirit can't balance naturally if you have toxic trapped emotions like anger, bitterness, resentment, failure, worthlessness, feelings of abandonment, etc. Trapped emotions are like nails in your spirit. Remove the nails and cleanse the wounds and they will naturally heal. Remove the trapped emotions and you will heal from the inside out.

Our common practice has been to treat the mind and body in order to heal the spirit. We have been doing it backward, thus getting backward results. If we focus on healing the spirit first, then healing the mind and body will naturally follow.

Fixing Spirit Issues

Many therapists only treat the mind and body, but they are limited by this approach because we are spiritual beings having a physical experience. Suicidal ideation is rooted in a pain not even a preacher, bishop, or rabbi can fix. I know because I went to my church leaders for help. I went to a therapist. I pushed for answers. They all threw up their arms not knowing how to help me. One therapist even admitted that he didn't know what to do for me. So who treats and heals the energy of the spirit? A certified energy practitioner.

Certified energy practitioners are specially trained for re-moving trapped emotions. There are many different modal-ities available. They release toxicity and raise spirit energy, increasing your consciousness level. When you release toxic energy, you repair unseen spiritual imbalances. This is when miracles begin. You will feel like a new person.

The thought of energy healing is outside the comfort zone for many, but it is time we seek new options. Anything that heals and makes you closer to your creator is divine. It has pure intent. It is your higher power reaching down and removing your pain. It's a beautiful thing. It is pure love in action. This healing is open to all regardless of religious beliefs or lack thereof.

Can It Help You?

We sometimes get lost in our modern world. Here's an example:

Imagine a teenager who appears to have all their needs met. They are living in a peaceful and nurturing home environment and getting along with both parents and siblings, a straight "A" student, living in abundance, very active in sports and/or band, and exhibits to be a happy person to those on the outside.

Why would a person like this ever consider taking their own life? Sadly, it happens all too often - but why?

Because their pain comes from somewhere deep and un-seen, a pain that may have been caused by past known or unknown trauma that has caused a blockage in energy flow. The mind, body, and spirit are out of harmony with one another. It is a blockage of self-love, an energy event that is stuck within the energy field of their spirit causing pain. It could be an inherited trapped emotion. People with self-love don't sabotage or destroy themselves.

Remember, every pain in life is here to teach and guide us. We have lost this wisdom of healing over the years but now it is back. Now that you have read this book, you now have the knowledge to do something to prevent your child or loved one from giving up on life.

They Will Not Talk to Me About It

The pains of the spirit create a feeling of lack, shame, guilt, and worthlessness greater than the body pain of a pinched nerve or a migraine headache. It is a continuous pain stuck inside the spirit that will not go away on its own.

There are reasons people with suicidal thoughts don't typically talk about these emotions and feelings. They want to talk but they don't understand what they are feeling. Traditional therapists are only trained to treat the mind and body. They are doing what they were trained to do, but when I tried to talk to therapists about it at the spirit level, most looked at me bug-eyed. From my experience, they didn't have a clue.

How could a person explain how they feel if they don't understand what they're feeling? And the person they are talking to doesn't understand it either. That is the darkness many are in. I believe the main reason suicidal individuals don't talk about it with parents or loved ones is that they don't know how to explain it. How does a teen know to tell a parent "I think my spirit is in pain."? If they did say that most people wouldn't know how to treat it anyway, but now you know.

I now realize there is a gap of understanding between therapists and religious leaders. Neither understood me but releasing the trapped emotions was the healing that I needed.

People Don't Want to Die

I am convinced that no one *wants* to die by suicide. They may lack joy or peace, believing they are unworthy, worthless, and unlovable. They feel flawed, broken, or they think that they are doing something wrong. They believe that peace is unavailable to them here on Earth. Today we have answers. We know that peace can be restored to the mind, body, and spirit and anybody can go on to live a fulfilled life.

My Observations

I have not completed any official scientific research on the most common causes of suicide. However, I have worked with diverse communities, from the homeless to presentation to audiences. Considering their observations and my own experience of struggles, and as an energy healer, it is my opinion that 99% of all those that considers suicide have one thing in common. Each of those suffering individuals had lost their connection to their source, their authentic self, the essence of who they are. As a result, they lost their life force and their will to live. Most had lost their connection through a single traumatic event or an ongoing environment of trauma like childhood abuse or toxic relationships. That is a testament to the importance of living an authentic life.

Realizing I was not connected to my authentic self was a major "Aha!" moment for me. *But what does that all mean?* you might ask. Simply, if you are experiencing suicidal thoughts, you are out of balance in mind, body, and spirit. You're not in harmony with your authentic self. The great news is now you know the problem's origin. If you know the root problem, you can fix it. The best news is with proper treatment you can immediately begin regaining balance by releasing trapped emotions, which will allow you to enjoy life and thrive in all you do. You can rid yourself of all the unseen emotional weight you are carrying in life.

When I experienced this rebalancing, it was like I finally figured out how to stop that "oil leak." I found the root cause. Then when I filled up my fuel tank, I had amazing energy to get through the day. When I stopped the leak by regaining balance in my inner and external life, it allowed my spirit to be filled with self-love and joy. My engine runs well these days because I have no oil leaks and unlimited fuel each day.

I now have unconditional love for others and for myself. With access to self-love, suicide will never again be an option for me.

Suicide is a Temporary Problem! Really?

The common saying that "suicide is a permanent solution for a temporary problem" is toxic. It's hogwash! Why? Because it encourages suicide. You heard me right. This saying demonstrates the typical disconnect between depressed or otherwise struggling people and those who want to help them. Suicidal people don't think their problems are temporary.

They feel their problems are permanent, which they are until the root problem is found and resolved.

All people struggling with their life force, their "will to live," believe this kind of pain may be temporary for everybody else, but not for them. They will then accept that they are the only one that feels it is permanent. Thus, creating more of an isolated person. Unless you've been there, you can't fully understand it. I have never met one person struggling that believed it was temporary.

Teach Proactive Suicide Prevention

Our primary goal should be proactive education to help those before struggling to recognize that suicide is never an option. Encourage them to save that into their belief system. If they know there is always help and healing available, that is a game changer. Suicidal thoughts do not mean you are weak. They indicate that you are out of balance. This distinction is part of a lesson.

We must teach them more effective ways to connect with themselves and others. Meditation is an effective practice for daily balance and is gaining more followers every day, but releasing trapped emotions is the fast lane on the road to healing from the inside out. Then meditation helps you to maintain balance.

There are Answers

Everything is simple once we understand it. When we understand it, we can do something about it.

A special note to therapists, counselors, doctors, teachers, clergy, social workers, halfway house managers, those that work with veterans, those from abusive homes, and anyone else who works with human beings that are struggling in life:

I encourage you to become a certified energy healing practitioner to help yourself and others. No degree is required. There is such a demand for this skill in our society and a shortage of those who can help.

Our ability to provide a service that heals is proportional to the richness we receive from our service. It is a win-win situation. Trapped emotions are recognized today by many doctors and therapists all over the world and are being recognized as necessitating treatment.

I encourage anyone working with people who struggle to look at energy healing as a viable treatment option. Anyone who has a desire to connect to his or her intuition can become a certified practitioner in energy healing. If you are struggling, you can still go through the certification process because that is healing in itself. Use energy healing alongside your current training and you will begin to see astounding results. You can become a master of healing.

Let's all work together to eliminate suicide.

Chapter Summary

Gratitude and suicidal thoughts do not coexist. Self-love and despair do not coexist. I released the toxic emotions of childhood abuse and look what happened! I went from struggling and barely surviving, making less than $15,000 a year for over 12 years, to making $1,000,000 my first full year back in the real estate business, making over 10 times that of the average agent.

I also attracted and connected with the love of my life, and we live in harmony with one another, never fighting, and always understanding each other. These pivotal changes both happened because of my desire to find answers and receive the type of healing I needed. Energy healing is the future.

Balance in wholeness and then all richness will be opened to you.

Joe Cox, Jr.

CHAPTER 14

Happiness as a Way of Life

To know how to attain happiness you must know what it is and how to attract it. Now you have the information you need to create the life you desire to live in a state of happiness no matter your background.

Happiness is not like a diet where you do it for a little while then go back to your old routine. Happiness is a way of living. It allows peace, joy, and harmony to guide your life and wards off chaos, suffering, and struggle.

You have the information to rid yourself of emotional turmoil. You can now heal yourself with an authentic, non-invasive healing method and receive effective results. You can now live the life you desire.

Remember to seek guidance from your intuition. Your mind thinks it knows what you want. Your intuition knows what you need. It will guide you to attract the most beneficial people into your life.

> ### *Stress is a result of living out of harmony with your authentic self.*
> *Joe Cox, Jr.*

As I mentioned, I left real estate after about 10 years in the business due to my personal struggles. Right after I started back in the business an associate asked, "Why did you go back into real estate? Wasn't that going backward?" I answered, "I didn't go back into real estate; I came back to finish the job I started." I didn't leave by choice. I needed to heal before I could continue. Remember, it's all a matter of perspective.

Many think, "I will be happy when...," sacrificing happiness today, thinking they are preparing to be happy in the future. If you are not happy today, you will not likely be happy in the future if you are still operating within the same detrimental belief system of delayed happiness. A healthier belief system says *I live in gratitude and well-being today while working on my wholeness and richness to attract abundance and happiness in all I do.*

Some people reading this may say, "It's too late for me. I'm too old." I say, *Hogwash!* If you are not where you want to be in life, that mindset is the reason why. The same actions will yield the same results.

In the first 20 years of life, you learn to walk, talk, read, write, and hopefully, you begin learning critical thinking skills. From 20-40 years of age, you learn street smarts, advanced education, more advanced life skills, and hopefully you learn who your real friends are. With this knowledge and toolbox of skills and wisdom, there is no limit to what you can do. Rather than going to look for just any job, design your life. You're never too old to change.

I started over at 50 years old. I know someone that started over at 65. The difference was all in the attitude. Remember, you are in it for the long haul. Wholeness is attained based on your belief system. It's never too late. You're not living for your body. You're living for your infinite self, and your infinite self never ages. Your life here is not done until you take your last breath.

I learned all these lessons the hard way and now I have handed you the knowledge that took me 40 years to gather. I have no regrets about my past because after walking through hell and back, I live an inspiring life full of meaning and purpose, so others like you can benefit from my experiences.

In Final Summary

Hopefully, life is becoming more clear for you. The steps in this book allowed me to attain and maintain happiness for the first time in my life. They allowed me to attract the person I needed to thrive at my greatest level in life.

Happiness comes first by gaining balance in wholeness. Gaining wholeness comes through achieving a balance of mind, body, and spirit through proper living and seeking meaning and purpose.

Simply put, your life is about you and your development within. Self-care is the priority so you can take care of those that you love.

The most important and fundamental step is self-love. Without self-love, nothing else matters. If you chase wealth without wholeness, you will be fighting a much more difficult battle. Most people that make wealth their priority will never attain it. Those that do will attempt to fill the needs of the inner self with material items. It never works. It can't. That's against nature. You can't cheat nature. You can't violate life's rules without consequences. Seek wholeness in all things first.

Richness is much easier to attain and maintain when you are balanced in wholeness. With wholeness, you attract abundance. With richness, you attract wealth as part of the balance in all things. Wholeness sets the stage for manifesting to work.

> *Look for the Lesson in All You Do.*
> *Be All You Can to be True.*
> *The Mistake is the Lesson,*
> *Now Look for the Question.*
> *Once it is Clear, You Have*
> *Nothing to Fear.*
>
> *Joe Cox, Jr.*

Happiness is not something you find but is a byproduct of inner wholeness, plus the level of richness that you desire from everything outside you. With wholeness and richness, you have everything you need for happiness to come to you and follow you wherever you go. This is completeness.

Now that you know this information, now that you know everything you need is within you, it almost seems too easy, right?

Set Your Life GPS

At a time I was struggling with inner turmoil, I came home one day to find that my wife had stippled over my closet door "You Got This". So, every morning before I get dressed I see those words. They help me to make sure I begin my day with an attitude of gratitude and remind me that I am in control of my life.

> *Happiness is not the purpose of life,*
> *Happiness is the reward for a life*
> *well lived.*
>
> Joe Cox, Jr.

The only reason we want money is for what we think it will give us within. Love, acceptance, memories, and experiences. But what do you really desire? You now see that with a balance in wholeness you are lacking nothing within. The irony of it all is once we don't crave the material things to define us, we easily receive an abundance of material things.

Remember, the only way you fail in life is if you quit life itself. You understand there is an answer for every situation and now you know how to find it. Remember to look for the lesson in all you do. Allow your intuition to guide you. Listen with your heart.

You are an infinite being with immeasurable value, born to create life by design. Trust yourself. Believe in yourself.

You now have the information you need to play the game of life and win. You know that Earth is a school for your infinite self. Life happens *for* you. When you play by and follow natural law, you will always win.

You are already the perfect you. Your goal is to become the best you.

I look forward to hearing from you how this book helped. No matter what you do in life, there is always an answer. So now you know to NEVER, EVER, EVER, GIVE UP!

I wish you much happiness and wealth in your life. Sending you blessings in all you do. From my heart to yours.

Made in the USA
Columbia, SC
01 November 2023

25322620R00102